The First of the Tide

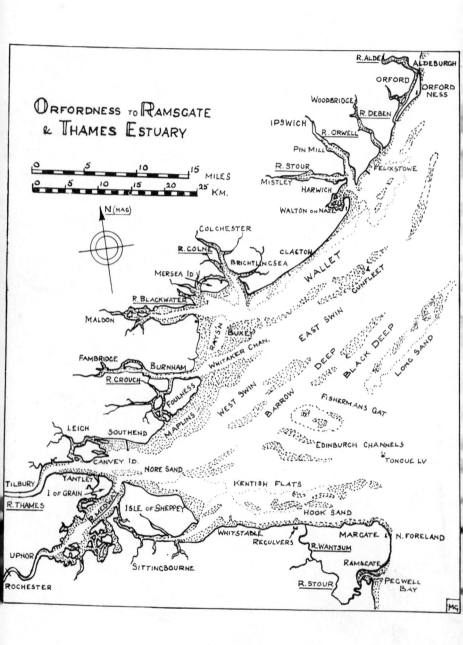

The First of the Tide

Reminiscences of East Coast Cruising

by
Maurice Griffiths

Illustrated by the author

Conway Maritime Press
Greenwich

Other Maurice Griffiths books available from
Conway Maritime

The Magic of the Swatchways
Dream Ships

©Maurice Griffiths 1979
First published in Great Britain 1979 by
Conway Maritime Press Ltd,
2 Nelson Road, Greenwich,
London, SE10 9JB

ISBN 0 85177 164 5

Typesetting by Industrial Artists Ltd, Hitchin
Printed in Great Britain by
Butler & Tanner Ltd, Frome

Foreword

When a man has passed his earthly allotted span he tends to look back over the years rather than forward. Ahead there appears little to look forward to, but in his wake, as it were, he can see all the events that have gone to make up his life. An old man's tendency, therefore, is to inflict on anyone who will stop and listen stories of days gone by, beginning with the inevitable 'I remember . . .'.

Some forty-seven years have elapsed since my first book of sailing reminiscences was launched under the title *The Magic of the Swatchways*. It was a simple collection of personal happenings in various little craft, mainly within the confines of the Estuary of the Thames and the Southern North Sea. But it had its appeal, evidently, to those who enjoy barging about in boats, for over the years it has reappeared in several editions.

Since then great changes have come over these same waters. There have been alterations to the channel buoys with the introduction of the International Association of Lighthouse Authorities, many of the old familiar beacons, like the Whitaker and the Nass, have acquired new shapes and top-marks, creeks and rivers are crowded with yachts' moorings, and packed yacht harbours and marinas have sprung up all round the coasts.

The yachting scene has indeed changed beyond all recognition since the Hitler war, not only in our home waters but in every part of the world where boat-minded people are able to follow their sport on the water. Countless thousands of couples, with and without children, now make their homes afloat in small yachts. So many make the voyage from the English Channel and ports of the Continent to the West Indies, the Caribbean and beyond each year, while others turn left at Gibraltar and spend years cruising the sea routes of the Phoenicians, the Romans and the Venetians throughout the Middle Sea, that long voyages in little yachts have become commonplace.

This explosion of ocean voyaging has come about through the introduction of automatic steering devices. By means of mechanical vane gears or electronic appliances the chief bugbear of the lone sailorman or the short-handed small sailing craft making lengthy passages is completely taken care of.

Like a model racing yacht uncannily keeping its course across a pond, the modern self-steering yacht can be left to stay on course for hours or days on end, so long as the wind serves, while her crew can sleep or go about the daily chores.

Such events as the Single-handed Transatlantic Race and Francis Chichester's astonishing round the world solo and other long voyages were made possible only by the introduction of self-steering devices. Women sailors, too, have not been slow to take advantage of man's ingenuity in this form. A number of women have not only competed in single-handed ocean races but, like Clare Francis, have made long voyages on their own, while the intrepid Naomi James completed a solo world circumnavigation non-stop in her 15-metre sloop in 1978.

With such breathtaking examples of what can be achieved by determined men and women in small cruising yachts, how trivial must seem the little adventures and delights of those who are content to sail their boats mainly within sight of the land. Yet, to countless thousands of boat loving people whose chief enjoyment is this pottering about in estuary waters — amidst shoals and sandbanks, withies and beacons, swatch-ways and creeks, and with the scents of the land mingling with the tang of the sea — such trivia can spell endless delight.

With chart and echo sounder (leadline or sounding pole) amidst all the crowds of other boats, quiet and peaceful anchorages are still to be discovered by those who seek solitude. This little book is accordingly offered in all humility as recollections of an old sailorman whose sailing days have generally been as simple as that.

MAURICE GRIFFITHS
West Mersea
Essex 1979

Contents

1   Groping in the dark   page 9
2   Every day's an adventure   19
3   Stranded on the Buxey   29
4   Nothing quite like a smack   41
5   Trouble on the bar   55
6   By the Havengore route   65
7   Slowly into the Swale   77
8   Calm off the Roman Coast   89
9   Tides are forces to reckon with   103
10 Two ways across the estuary   115
11 If we are where we think . . .   127
12 Cruising is what you make it   141

1

Groping in the dark

As dusk began to darken the sea the last whispers of the breeze died away. The burgee at the masthead no longer even fluttered but hung limp from its angled stick, and as the tide, which had been such a friendly help all afternoon, paused and then turned to run its course northwards again, the little sloop with her pram-bowed dinghy astern began to drift back, little by little.

There was nothing for it, then, but to let go the anchor, stow the sails and wait. Clambering into the pram, I spent some time rowing quietly round the little ship, admiring her from all angles with the ardour of a lover in the early stages of a romance. That she was not an arresting beauty as yachts go, that there was nothing about her to suggest a gentleman's yacht from the Solent, bothered me not at all: she was recently mine, and that drew a gloss over most of her failings.

Seventeen feet not counting the five-foot bowsprit, lapstrake or clinker-built with a plain straight stem and upright transom stern, she had spent much of a humble life lashed on to the skids on the after deck of a North Sea trawler; then someone with unquenchable enthusiasm for such projects had bought her on the dockside, removed the rowing thwarts, and fitted her with a lead keel, a deck and coamings and a small cabin with a lifting coachroof and canvas sides. He had rigged her with a short mast hinged on deck in a tabernacle (so that she could pass under bridges) and standing lug mainsail and jib, and set her to do hire work on the Broads. So this common ship's boat had risen in life to become a proper little yacht, taking sailing parties about the Norfolk rivers until the Great

War ended and larger and much sleeker yachts could be built to take the place of such as she was, poor thing.

Dabchick, as she was called when I bought her, was the very first boat I had possessed on my own, for the smack-like cutter two pals and I had shared the previous summer had not been a complete success, and after the dissolution of the partnership I had bought this sloop at Woodbridge for the modest sum of thirty pounds in the spring of 1922. And here I was now on my own with everything about cruising still to learn.

Night was already spreading over the sky and darkening the sea, and as I rested on the oars, allowing the pram to drift silently past the anchored yacht on the first of the ebb, the lamps along the promenade at Clacton suddenly sprang into life in groups like the lighted windows of a long train awaiting the 'right away' whistle from the guard. This, some two miles short of the pier, was as far as today's sail had brought us until the fitful wind had failed altogether with the end of the daylight.

It had in truth taken *Dabchick* most of the day to work down the Orwell from her home mooring outside the lock gates at Ipswich. The wind had been light and hesitant from the south east from the start, blowing gently straight up the lovely wooded river, and however eager my ship's-boat-turned-Broads-holiday-yacht might have been to get down to the sea, my own ineptitude as a helmsman showed up markedly at sailing her close-hauled on her zig-zag course to windward.

Abreast the weathered red brick Tudor tower at Freston was one of the many places in this narrow channel where the previous summer my equally inexperienced partners and I — who, let's face it, was at the helm at the time — ran our 6-tonner aground on the ebb. And here we had spent several hours perched on the edge of a deck that sloped at fifty degrees while one Ipswich yacht after another sailed gaily past in the sunshine of a glorious summer's day packed, it seemed, with friends wearing grins a foot wide. Pretending to admire the scenery we tried to ignore such pleasantries as 'Diggin' for bait, Griff?' or 'Hello, found the putty *again*?' but it's difficult to maintain an air of dignity and command of the situation at that angle while the world passes by.

So it was on this day when with *Dabchick* I cautiously made only short tacks, keeping well away from the hidden mud banks on each side, although I knew her draught was but three feet and barely more than half that of our old cutter. Past the woods at Woolverstone and the Inkpot, the black buoy off Cathouse Point, we beat our way tack by tack down the river and through the crowds of yachts on moorings off Pin Mill, like a climber working up the side of the foothills of a mountain.

At the moorings in Butterman's Bay, the reach just below Pin Mill, a great four-masted barque was unloading grain through chutes over her rusty side into lighters and barges. *Lawhill* was one of the ships which were too large to negotiate the narrow channel farther up to the docks at Ipswich, and from these ship moorings in Butterman's Bay the cargo would be sailed up in the tan-sailed spritsail barges, or towed by a tug in the lighters.

The day was proving fine and the breeze warm and friendly, and as we progressed down Sea Reach making alternate long and short legs, Harwich Harbour lay before us, and suddenly opening out beyond and sparkling in the afternoon sunshine was — the sea! I found myself singing lustily to the gulls which were tracing sweeping gestures against the blue of the sky overhead, for I had managed to take at short notice — too short for any of my friends to join me — a week's leave from the estate agent's office where I was then working. It is probable that they were relieved to be rid of me, but that didn't worry me unduly, for here I was free, with my own little boat, heading out of the harbour for the first time alone.

As the ancient naval port slid past to starboard, with its central church spire, the roof of the Three Cups hotel where Nelson stayed, and the seventeenth century high and low lighthouses which no longer pointed the way in through the present channel, the sand cliffs of the Naze began to open out over the bowsprit end, and I felt the adventure had begun. Every sailing man must experience the thrill of his first attempt to put out to sea in his own little boat, and recall every minute of it, however trivial the event might appear in distant retrospect.

The tall brick tower, erected by Trinity House in 1720 as a landmark for mariners approaching this somewhat featureless coast, drew abreast and the pier at Walton opened out through the lee rigging. The low coastline stretching away towards the south west held as much promise to me as the headlands of the West Coast of Africa for Prince Henry the Navigator's captains when they sailed their caravels from the rocky shore of Sagres on and ever on, southward in their search for a sea route to the fabulous East. For the beginner in his little craft this modest 15 mile stretch of water between the coast and the Gunfleet sands some three and a half miles to seaward, which was shown on my chart as the Wallet, beckoned with its wavelets glinting in the sun.

In the next few days, if the fates were kind to a simple sailor, this course would lead my little ship to places like Brightlingsea and Wivenhoe and the Colne, to West Mersea and up the Blackwater to Heybridge and Maldon; and I mused we might, the fates and weather permitting, sail through the Ray Sand channel into the mouth of the Crouch and, venturing while the tide served, arrive at Burnham, the Mecca of East Coast yachtsmen as I had heard it described. Then there were more places farther up the river, at Fambridge, Hullbridge and Battlesbridge, while by taking a left turn just inside the Crouch into what the chart marked as the River Roach I saw that we could come to Paglesham and the Broomhill river, and a group of islands around Havengore. But as yet, all these places were for me but names printed on the chart.

When the smart houses at Frinton and the low gap at Holland-on-Sea had slowly dropped astern it became clear that our friendly breeze was dying of boredom, and as her sails began to fall in limp folds of time-worn canvas it seemed that *Dabchick* was tiring of the day's efforts. Perhaps in these light airs she felt the drag of the dinghy she had been towing all day, and who could blame her, seeing that the little nine-foot boat was more than half the length of the yacht towing her?

In these highly mechanised days when even the smallest yachts carry lightweight plastic dinghies shaped like overgrown soap dishes, or with inflatables resembling black rubber doughnuts hauled snub-nosed on to the stern guardrail, it does seem incredible that almost every yacht under about forty feet, of the time of which we are speaking, should regularly tow a wooden dinghy too big and heavy to carry on deck. But in 1922 very few of our little yachts of less than, say, 32 feet in length had what was then called an auxiliary motor. With no handy power to roar into action at the press of a button, as is expected nowadays, running aground and having to kedge off, or laying out the bower anchor with its cable, was a common occurrence. The yacht's tender therefore had to be man enough to carry out kedge and warp or anchor and chain, perhaps in very choppy conditions, without sinking. *Dabchick*'s clinker-built pram had been included in the sale for a further £6 — a reasonable enough price for a nearly new nine-footer at that date — and if she was over-large for a 17-footer to tow, I was to be glad of the little vessel's ability as a service boat more than once before the season was out.

Clambering back on board, I lit the oil lamp in the cabin and sat for a few minutes looking around with a feeling of pride at the warm tints reflected in the varnish work, at the cunningly arranged cooking locker with its primus stove, and the natty little shelves. And when I had the stove roaring and the cabin filling with the seductive smell of eggs and bacon, *Dabchick*'s kennel-like cabin became charged with such warmth and homeliness that I wouldn't have changed places with any man in England.

'Dabchick' always towed a pram dinghy

The calm continued while the ebb tide sucked past the planks of the anchored hull, and in the euphoria that follows hours of activity and a substantial meal I got my head down on the starboard berth for a few hours' sleep. Bringing up, letting go the hook, and waiting for the tide to turn or a breeze to spring up has been a part of the sailorman's life through countless ages; it was the way sailors worked their unhandy vessels with cargoes around all the coasts of the world.

Shipmen of the Middle Ages in their round-bellied ships, like cogs and nefs, cats and herring busses rigged with simple square sails, knew all the tricks of working their tides, the eddies and patches of slack water, as well as the changing winds, in their voyagings between the North Sea harbours and the Hansa ports of the Baltic. As soon as the tide came foul, over went old Cold Nose on its hempen cable, down came the sails, and there the ship would wait until the tide was done or a fair wind sprang up.

Even in the early nineteenth century days of the East Coast coal trade, the collier brigs and brigantines, schooners and billyboys might be held up for days, weeks in winter, by strong southerly gales, until seacoals in London and in all the coastal ports would rise to famine prices. Capable as many of these little vessels might be at clawing to windward with the tide under them, few of them could work over the ground against both a wind and a tide. The yachtsman in his engine-less craft was in the same position, and come a calm or a fluky breeze ahead and a foul tide he could do nothing but bring up and wait. And that is precisely what I had had to do in *Dabchick*.

The merry trickle-trickle sound that you hear inside a clinker-built boat when the wind first stirs the ripples had me awake in a trice. My watch said it was five minutes short of midnight, and I reckoned it must be nearly low water. Outside in the cockpit the night was pitch dark with an overcast sky and not a star showing, and I found that a light breeze was filling in from about south west.

The long train of lamps still shone fingers of light quivering across the water from Clacton, while to seaward the red glare of the Gunfleet pile lighthouse on the other side of the sands stabbed the darkness at minute intervals. The only other light that I could see was ahead, and far enough away to be almost dipping on the horizon as I stood in the cockpit. When I climbed on to the cabin top it became clearer and I was able to count its flashes — a white light every ten seconds. That, the chart told me, would be the Knoll buoy off the mouth of the Colne and about four miles away.

Even as I watched, the Clacton lights went out in groups as they had appeared, until there was no visible sign of life along the shoreline in either direction. Suddenly it seemed distinctly lonesome out here on the dark bosom of the Wallet, and an involuntary shiver ran down my spine as I felt how chill the breeze was, and I dived below to put on warmer clothes.

While I crouched on knees under the low cabin top struggling into the clinging roughness of a jersey, a shower of raindrops pattered on the deck like distant machine-gun fire, and with it the noise of the wavelets under the lands of the planking told me the breeze was increasing in earnest. Recalling the old mariner's rhyme read in some book or other:

> *When the rain comes afore the wind*
> *Tops'l sheets and haulyards mind.*
> *When the wind comes afore the rain*
> *Soon you will set sail again!*

I decided that whichever had arrived first, and that seemed uncertain, I should be wise to tie a reef in the mainsail (why I hadn't been prudent enough to do that immediately after anchoring, like any wise sailorman, I couldn't tell), and get underway for some sheltered anchorage in case it came on to blow.

The candle in the compass box was lit, and with the anchor once more catted in the bow fairlead, one reef tucked in the mainsail and a smaller jib set, *Dabchick* was soon scrunching into the choppy seas as she tacked towards the Knoll light, the bluff bow of the pram bash-bashing in her wake. The flash of the Knoll was steadily growing brighter through the rain as we drew nearer, and soon the gaunt cage itself could be made out between flashes as the buoy reeled past and the sound of the tide washing past its rusty sides confirmed that the first of the flood was already running in our favour.

For a time I pored over the chart in the dim light of the compass, pondering whether to bear away to leeward and run up the Colne for the remainder of the night. But the Knoll light was already well astern and the night appeared more than ever as dark as a cow's inside, there was no light, not even a barge's riding light, to show where the anchorage was, while the chart showed that the channel became narrower as it went up, and I didn't fancy running blind before this breeze.

As the wind was broad on the port bow if I kept the boat heading towards West Mersea I decided to keep her on a course of roughly NW by W, for there appeared on the chart a good anchorage inside Mersea Quarters with a wide entrance without any bar and a beacon on the spit of land called the Nass for a guide. Although the wind was not increasing so far, and was just a nice whole sail breeze, it was still raining and with such little visibility I reckoned this was about the safest course to take.

For a chart I was using the only one then available to yachtsmen in these waters, a slender, green-covered volume which had been a welcome Christmas present — after a little nudging — from an understanding aunt. It was Lt S C Messum's *East Coast Rivers* which had appeared in 1903, and in the manner of the well known Frank Cowper's *Sailing Tours* series, published a decade or more before, it had coloured charts drawn by the author. With helpful sailing directions in the text it was a blessing for the inexperienced boat sailor in these waters between London's river and Orfordness.

Between the Knoll and Mersea Quarters the chart showed there were three unlighted buoys which were roughly on the route — the Eagle, the North West Knoll and the Bench Head — and I kept a wary eye out in case I should crash into one, but peer as I might through the rain I didn't catch a glimpse of any one of them. This began to worry me, for I knew that somewhere through the murk to leeward the beach of Mersea Island must lie, but there was no sign of it, not a light to be seen anywhere, just wet blackness and the steady hiss of the bow wave and the patter of rain in the mainsail.

With her long straight keel *Dabchick* had all the comforting characteristics of the old time straight-stemmed yacht in keeping steadily on her course, and I had already learnt the art of letting her sail herself with a line and slip hitch holding the tiller. So now I was glad to leave my little boat to grope her way through the night while I crouched in the lee side of the cockpit and took an occasional sounding with the five fathom leadline. But as yet the lead failed to touch bottom.

I was beginning to wonder if the compass card swimming in the soft candlelight was leading me astray through some deviation I had not suspected, and that unsettling doubt that we might be steering quite the wrong course crept over me, as at times it has done to mariners through countless ages. The Knoll had dropped so far astern that its flash was no longer visible: either the rain was blotting it out or its light had already dipped below the horizon, so even that check on our course had disappeared, and I peered around and back at the compass with a distrustful eye.

Rather than give way to temptation and set a new panic course, however, I allowed common sense to prevail with the belief that there was no deviation matter close to the compass card — a knife, steel marlinespike or large iron shackle for instance — to affect it, and with the thought that *Dabchick* knew what she was doing I held her on the NW by W line. It was almost two hours since we passed the Knoll and I knew we must be closing in with the Nass beacon by now. Messum described the beacon as a substantial post, and I constantly peered through the murk ahead hoping we should not sail bang into it. Later I was to learn that the name was called locally *Narce,* a Danish word meaning a sand spit, and we all know how prone the Danes around these parts were to speak with very refined accents!

With the next cast the lead found bottom at three and a half fathoms, then three, followed shortly after with two and a half. We could not be far off the shore now, I reckoned, and before soundings became less and we sailed ourselves on to the mud somewhere I cast off the tiller line, rounded up into the wind, dropped mainsail and jib as smartly as maybe, and let go the hook with ten fathoms of chain.

It was still raining, and as soon as I had the sails properly furled and the hurricane lamp hung up on the forestay as a riding light, I was glad to dive into the cabin, wriggle out of the wet clothes, and turn into my berth with the warm satisfaction of having achieved a first time passage round the coast without, so far, disaster. In a few hours, daylight would show just where we had got ourselves to.

2

Every day's an adventure

Bright sunshine slanting into the cabin had me awake and out into the cockpit. The night's rain had gone and I gazed around enraptured with the scene: the wide Blackwater glinting under a clear sky to the south west, and on the other side of the boat the wooded high ground of Mersea Island with the squat tower of the church rising above the trees. It looked an enchanting place.

'Well done, Dabby! You found your way in after all.'

I couldn't resist giving my little boat's coaming an affectionate slap as my eyes caught sight of the tall post of the Nass a half mile to seaward, with a cormorant, wings outstretched drying in the sun like a black statue, motionless on the barrel top. We had sailed past the beacon unseen in the darkness, and here we were at anchor well inside the Quarters in about as good a place as one could wish. *Dabchick* knew what she was doing all right.

The channels leading up to the Hard between sedge covered banks seemed to be full of smacks and yachts of all descriptions, and I noticed that several of them were hoisting coloured pennants as though dressing ship for some event. After breakfast I couldn't wait to put the water jar in the dinghy and row up the channel between Cobmarsh Island and the tarred oyster packing shed standing on blocks on the top of Packing Marsh on the west bank.

Prominent amongst all the craft in the other creeks were the oyster smacks. Although I was already familiar with the sight of the shrimping bawleys working off Harwich, with their big topsails and boomless mainsails, their broad transom sterns and chimneys smoking when the catch was being boiled, yet I had never seen so many smacks together before. I was to learn later on that there were usually between fifty and sixty of these handsome vessels based at Mersea, and many more to be found round at Brightlingsea in the Colne, and more still up the Blackwater at Maldon.

Fine craft they appeared to be, ranging from 30ft to 42ft (9.1–12.8m) in length, with immensely long bowsprits and mainbooms reaching out beyond the square counter stern, bulwarks almost knee high surrounding the broad decks, and the low freeboard aft needed by the smacksmen for handling the oyster drudges or hauling the great beam trawl. Working in groups off Colne Point, in the Wallet, or farther afield in the Swin, the Mersea smacks were to become as familiar a sight as the tan-sailed spritsail barges from London River.

At the top of the Hard I found a group of fisherman actively engaged in erecting a tall pole on the foreshore in front of a row of fisherman's cottages. 'Thas the greasy pole,' one of them told me. 'Allus hev that every regatta day. Have a goo, bor, when it's ready?' So that accounted for the bunting on some yachts and the general excitement that I felt in the air.

Looking around I also noticed a big grey barge lying in the saltings, called *Molliette*. She looked like one of the con-

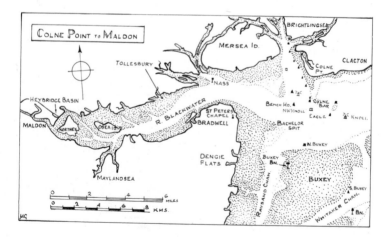

crete vessels which had been built during the war, and was now dressed overall with pennants fluttering in the breeze, and from a notice board by her gangway I could read that she was the headquarters of the West Mersea Yacht Club. To my query where to fill up my water jar another of the fisherman good-naturedly directed me. 'Do yew goo along Coast Road, bor, to St Peter's well,' he said. 'Thas good spring water, that is. Make your hair curl, that it will.'

Along the sandy lane beyond the cottages near the Hard I passed oyster breeding ponds cut into the saltings and fishermen's huts, and farther on a few old black-hulled yachts with grotesque structures on deck, leaning slightly in their mud berths while they finished their days as houseboats. In the side of the sandy bank that bordered the lane I came across a spring trickling out of a pipe. This seemed to be the water supply the men spoke of, for there was already another yacht's water breaker underneath and brimming over. I moved the wooden barrel to one side and left my jar to fill.

In due time the fisherman's remark gained understanding, for I found that Mersea spring water had a flavour that likened it in the polite sense to spa water. In tea, especially, it was very much an acquired taste for the stranger to the island, and I think until a new water supply was piped on to the island only the locals were fully used to its taste.

Looking back over the years one cannot but recall how relatively primitive were the boats that we younger and more impecunious cruising men sailed in those days. Few of the type of small craft we could afford to buy and maintain — from clinker-built converted lifeboats to turn-of-the-century cutters and yawls, old fishing craft or little barge yachts — few of our craft, I recall, had such a domestic amenity as a fixed water tank. Fresh water was usually carried in two-gallon stone jars, like the one I was using which once held gingerbeer and was heavy enough even when empty; and we had to hump them on our shoulders back to the dinghy.

There were then no lightweight plastic containers, not even jerrycans, which didn't appear until the Hitler war: the only alternative to specially made and expensive galvanised cans was the standard two-gallon petrol tin which the motorist carried as a spare strapped to his running board outside the

driver's door. But these petrol tins (costing four shillings, 20p)
tended fairly soon to rust and discolour the water. Some
yachts carried oak brass-bound breakers (barricoes in naval
craft) which crews humped on their shoulders against bent
necks.

The small yacht's galley was also primitive enough: often
only a shelf in the fo'c's'le, copying the traditional layout plan
of the gentleman's yacht which had been designed to carry at
least one paid hand who would do all the cooking in the
fo'c's'le. If the galley in the modest 6-tonner was situated aft
of the cabin it was seldom more elaborate than a cupboard
with a primus slung in gimbals. One 7-tonner I later sailed
aboard was thought to have luxury in its cooking
arrangements, for inside a large locker at the after end of the
cabin were a gimballed primus for quick boiling and a
Rippingille stove which boasted a roasting oven between two
blue flame wick stoves. A variation of this, at least until the
Second World War, was the Clyde Cooker, a highly practical
oven stove made of brass-trimmed galvanised sheet metal,
with two primus burners incorporated, and marketed by
Messrs Simpson-Lawrence of Glasgow.

In our boats a sink with an outboard drain was unheard of,
while very few yachts under about 30ft (9.1m) or so were
blessed — or otherwise — with a flushing sea toilet. For the
likes of us the handy bucket, or galvanised sanitation as we
called it, was the norm for instant hygiene. The rig and gear of
our boats had also not changed radically since the schooner
America took the famous Cup back to the United States in
1851. Sails were cotton, while some of the large old timers still
sailed with flax, running gear was usually plain or lightly
tarred hemp or, aboard smart yachts and racing boats, cotton.
Many of our boats still set up the rigging with deadeyes and
lanyards, although all more recent yachts were using rigging
screws or turnbuckles.

Our elderly yachts were, in short, similar in many features
to the smacks, and with our long straight keels a ten- or
twelve-foot bowsprit was common enough. To hold this spar
from bending and snapping off at the stem from the weight of
a full swigged up jib, it had to have shrouds at the sides as well
as a chain bobstay leading down to the stem near the water-

line. On some boats with narrow bows the bowsprit shrouds were given a wider spread by means of a pair of athwartship whiskers, similar in principle to the spreaders or crosstrees which increase the angle of the masthead shrouds. The chain bobstay usually had a tackle led to the bowsprit end — the crans iron — so that it could be released and hauled up to the stemhead with a light line and so avoid the rasping and chafe against the cable while at anchor.

Jibs were usually set flying on an iron ring traveller which was hauled out to the end of the bowsprit by an outhaul line. Major Wykeham-Martin had introduced his ingenious and excellent jib roller furling gear back in 1903, and it was a godsend aboard many yachts to be able to unfurl or furl the jib by a tripping line from the cockpit; but few of us young beginners could afford such an expensive refinement — even had we known about it at the time.

Apart from the racing yachts of various classes, with their overhanging U-sectioned bows (they were known as spoon bows) and long counter sterns, needed to enable the crew to reach the end of the overhanging boom when reefing, most of the cruising yachts I had met so far in my travels were of the straight stem type with short counter or transom sterns. There were still a few with fiddlehead or clipper bows, but they were regarded as hopelessly old-fashioned, graceful though some of them appeared to our eyes. Fashions in yachts, as in other things, have a habit of repeating themselves, and it is entertaining to notice that in the year I am writing (1979) the so-called clipper bow with a modest, but often clumsy and ill-conceived, piece of scrollwork has returned to favour at Boat Shows amongst some sophisticated and highly expensive fibreglass creations.

The races had already started when I got back to the dinghy with the filled water jar, and it was engaging to find preparations in hand for a duck punt race. Unlike the decked punts of the Norfolk marshes these grey-painted Essex flatties, sixteen to eighteen feet long and as narrow as a cigar, set a big lugsail and were steered by a paddle held over the side in the traditional manner of the ancient mariners before the rudder was invented in the twelfth century. There were about a dozen working up to the start line off the Hard, and I was told they were all proper workaday wildfowler's punts, nothing special, mind you.

A tall figure in thigh boots, blue jersey and battered peaked cap above a full white beard and twinkling eyes, was pointed out to me. 'Thas Admiral Wyatt, that is,' one of the fisherman told me. 'Reckon he'll be champion agin this year, that I dew.'

Having always tended to be somewhat naïve and willing to believe everything I was told (almost), I thought, as I watched the punts shoot away down Mersea Fleet when the gun went, how surprising it was to learn that a high ranking naval officer should have come to Mersea to show the locals how to sail their punts. But in due time I was to get to know Bill Wyatt well as a great local character and builder of these punts (who should know them better than he?) as well as larger boats in his black shed by the Hard, and who was to prove invariably kind and helpful towards us hard up young sailors. The Wyatt family, I was to learn, had been in the boat- and shipbuilding business for generations, having built ships for the Navy at Buckler's Hard in Hampshire until the launching ways had become too restricted for the larger war-ships required after Nelson's day. The Wyatts had then emigrated to Essex, settled in the little fishing village on Mersea Island, and there prospered as boatbuilders and fishermen.

Reluctant to leave the gay hubbub of regatta day and the sports of boxing with flourbags on a plank, climbing the greasy pole, and all the fun that a local fair threatened to provide that evening, I was more concerned to take the last of this tide up the Blackwater. After we had tacked out and rounded the Nass, squaring away before the south easterly, it was clear that the breeze was becoming shy and fitful. To sea-ward groups of white racers had their topsails set while another class were running back with white spinnakers boomed out to one side like flying swans.

By the time the pier at Tollesbury had drawn abeam there was scarcely enough breeze left to hold the mainboom out, we had only just steerage way, and the merry chuckle of our pro-gress sank to an occasional murmur; but the flood tide was still urging us along little by little.

Gazing across the still water at the pier I could not help contemplating the strange things big companies sometimes do in the search for profit and progress. This substantial jetty and the single line that ran on to it were one of the old Great Eastern Railway's mistakes. The idea had been to build here a loading jetty having a rail link with the London—Ipswich—Norwich main line which would encourage steamers engaged in the Baltic timber and other Continental trades to discharge here instead of in London River. The Kelvedon, Tiptree and Tollesbury Light Railway was built to the pier and a service run, but beyond the jam-producing village of Tiptree the line proved a white elephant. Nobody had pointed out to the Directors that for an unloading berth the pier was on the wrong side, the lee side, of the river in all the prevailing south-westerly winds, and in time the railway was torn up.

Had the Great Eastern instead carried its Wickford to Burnham-on-Crouch line an additional five miles beyond its Southminster terminus to reach Bradwell, it has often been thought that they could have opened up the creek inside Pewit Island and built sheltered and profitable berths under its lee for small North Sea steamers. It took the building of a nuclear power station on the site, plus a yacht marina, half a century later to show how the creek could have been developed.

Past the beacon on Thirstlet Spit, where the river is a mile and three quarters wide at high water, but rather less than half that in the channel, the breeze died completely. The burgee hung limp and the parts of the mainsheet drooped to kiss their own reflections in the still water. Even the dinghy had fallen silent as the yacht steadily lost steerage way and continued to drift silently on the tide.

There was barely an hour's flood left to high water, and I was not keen to bring up so far from any landing when the ebb set in against us. The chart, according to Messum, showed a good anchorage just below the pier on the south side of Osea Island, and that was not more than three miles ahead. But we should never reach it at this rate.

A little exercise on the sweep was the obvious answer and, sliding the blade of the oar from its stowage place through the starboard shroud lanyards, I swung it in its crotch on the rail and began to lean my weight on the loom end with steady

25

strokes. The ton and a half that *Dabchick* weighed was child's play to get moving, and soon we were progressing through the water at an estimated two knots, while the tree-covered island came perceptibly closer.

In the days before yachts, smacks, barges, or indeed any small sailing craft had such a contrivance as an engine, the sweep — the wooden tawps'l as the bargemen called it — was as essential a piece of equipment as the anchor. All small yachts carried a sweep, usually a springy ash oar ten or twelve feet in length, even some of those fitted with a petrol or paraffin motor, for these pieces of ironmongery were far from reliable when needed in a hurry. The wooden topsail not only got a yacht along in a calm, but if a yacht was in danger of drifting down on to another anchored vessel, a ship's mooring buoy or even a shoal, a few strokes with the sweep would soon work her clear of the danger. The way bargemen manoeuvred a laden barge into a tight berth when the sails were useless by working their sweep over the bow was a commonplace example to us sailing men.

Working a yacht's sweep was not by any means the labour many of today's yachtsmen seem to imagine. There was no straining of the arm muscles as in the pictures of galley slaves in a sea fight. The sweep was usually well balanced in its rail crotch, and standing in the cockpit facing forward you just leant your chest on the oar for each stroke, up and back, dip, lean forward, up and back and so on. At first a heavy eight- or ten-ton yacht might seem reluctant to get moving, but once you had some way on, it was no punishment to keep at it for an hour or more on end. It was the way many yachts returned on the Sunday evening's tide to their home moorings in a flat calm.

As we came slowly up to the anchorage two yachts brought up near the pier were already on the swing. The fair tide was done, and soon the ebb would be running strongly back towards the sea. But *Dabchick* had won her minor race with the tide and, stowing the trusty sweep back along the footrail, I let go old Cold Nose in three fathoms not far off the sandy beach.

Osea Island, a mile and a quarter in length and half a mile across, had once been owned by a member of the Charrington family of brewers who apparently agreed so little with his family's trade that he had a handsome red brick house built on the island as a home for inebriates. It is said that local fishermen and others from Maldon reaped a goodly trade with some of the inmates by hiding caches of liquor where they could be collected.

During the Kaiser war the island had been used by the Admiralty as a coastal motor boat base, and when I landed from the dinghy I found the remains of the extensive concrete pond in which the two types of 40ft and 55ft CMB could be floated and tested. There was also at that time a small general store where I was able to buy fresh eggs and other provisions, while it was a sharp reminder that this was an island from the notice I found on the post box:

THE NEXT COLLECTION WILL BE SUBJECT TO THE TIDE

On the other side of the island a rough track marked by a line of rotting stakes ran half a mile across the Stumble to the north bank of the river, and it was evident that this would be covered for at least six hours of each tide. From a high part of the island I was able to see the great stretch of the river from Tollesbury and Bradwell past where I stood on its way up towards the hilly ground behind Maldon. Not quite so beautiful as the wooded winding reaches of the Orwell, yet this river was far more extensive, and I longed to explore every part of it. The Blackwater was, in fact, to be my principal sailing ground for over fifty years.

Above low water mark and not far from the pier was a lofty post, massive enough to have been shaped from the trunk of a great tree, which I was later to learn was known as the Barnacle and had been set at this spot to enable Bentall's yacht *Jullanar* to lie against it for scrubbing. The *Jullanar* was a milestone in yachting history, and was to influence the design of racing yachts over the next hundred years. She had been built in 1875 by E H Bentall, a manufacturer of agricultural machinery whose grey brick factory still stands beside the Chelmer Canal where it flows under the Colchester road bridge at Heybridge.

Bentall had been impressed with the experiments the naval architect William Froude had been making with ship models for the Admiralty in a test tank built in the garden of his home near Torquay. Froude had discovered certain hydro-dynamic laws governing ships' behaviour and performance at sea, amongst them that the drag of the water, skin friction he called it, passing along the ship's bottom accounted for almost all the resistance, and consequently the power needed to propel the ship (with steam or with sail) at lower speeds before bow waves and a stern wash were created. Realizing from his own sailing experience that most of the time when racing yachts were moving only slowly and making little wash, Bentall argued that one must reduce the area of the hull, the amount of wetted surface, below the waterline as much as possible, by cutting away all unnecessary deadwood.

The *Jullanar* was the result, by today's standards a very big yacht. Rigged as a conventional yawl, she was 126 tons TM, 111ft (33.8m) on deck, 100ft (30.5m) on the waterline, with 16.8 (5.1m) beam and drawing only 18in at her cutaway forefoot to 13.5ft (4.1m) aft. Her revolutionary profile was to affect the work of leading designers resulting in G L Watson producing first the extreme racer *Thistle,* and then the Prince of Wales' *Britannia* in 1893. The designer's aim to reduce to a minimum the wetted surface of a yacht's hull is to be noted in today's racing machines with their brief fin keels and separate rudders and orange-pip shaped bodies.

Bentall never himself raced *Jullanar,* by the way, for he was too interested in following her up with even more extreme hull designs, but with her later owner she proved a consistent winner against the long-keeled yawls and cutters of the day. It is recorded that the less sporting owners began to refuse to sail their yachts in any race if the dreaded *Jullanar* was entered. It seems they quarrelled over racing even in the 1870s!

Knowing nothing of these historical events at this time I rowed back to the modest *Dabchick* just to sit in contentment in the cockpit and admire the view while the ebb gurgled past in the mirror-like calm. Tomorrow morning, I promised my boat, we would take the flood tide when it served and sail up past Northey Island and the entrance to Heybridge Basin lock, and see for ourselves what kind of a port was Maldon.

3

Stranded on the Buxey

It was nearly high water and the right time to start, but I hung on to my anchor undecided what to do. After the past few days of sailing in light to moderate breezes, a depression had come in with an overcast sky, and the wind was now blowing hard from the south west — too hard, I felt, for a seventeen-foot boat to set off for home in weather like this. But this delay in my programme was setting a problem, for my week's holiday was nearly up and I ought to be back on the moorings and in the office by tomorrow morning.

Yet, here we were lying at anchor under the lee of the south bank at Burnham-on-Crouch, with all those miles back to Colne Point, through the Wallet, and up the Orwell to Ipswich still to do. And here it was blowing half a gale, admittedly a fair wind for the passage, but for me too darn much of it.

I kicked myself for leaving it so late so far from home, just through trying to pack too much cruising into seven days. It would be a lesson to remember on all future cruises — always to allow just one extra day for getting back, in case the weather breaks or some accident to boat or gear delays you. Ah, so. And like all thoroughly practical resolutions it was one I was to ignore more than once in the years to come; and more than once with chagrin!

Dabchick and I had spent two wonderful days in the Blackwater, sailing on the tide up to the fascinating waterfront at Maldon, where there were local smacks lying along the fore-shore below the church with the pointed spire. Farther up nearer the iron road bridge were six barges in a row at the berths, their sprits gleaming gold in the sunshine, lengthy bobs waving at their mastheads. Just astern of them against the wharf lay a handsome white cutter, a real old timer with straight stem and square counter stern like a smack's. When I edged *Dabchick* alongside a ricketty jetty at Dan Webb's yard I was told the cutter was the *Ripple*, 25 tons, and had been built here at Howard's yard in 1877, and kept in the Sadd family ever since.

It was at this yard, I also learnt, that the *Scoter*, a fine, big, beamy, centreboard cutter with a transom stern, which I had often admired on a mooring next to my own at Ipswich, had been built in 1894. I did not know then that this gaff cutter was to influence my ideas for designing shallow draught cruising yachts for many years to come.

Here along Maldon waterfront, and a mile down river at Heybridge Basin, there were scores of yachts I had never seen before, as well as numerous smacks and barges to be looked over. No wonder I had dallied for two whole days in the Blackwater, making friends with local sailing men and barge skippers, and old 'Dreamy' Austin the river pilot, before *Dabchick* took the flood tide southwards again through the Ray Sand channel (the Rays'n) into the Couch.

And then, sailing all day as the tides served we worked our way up the Roach to Paglesham, where in Shuttlewood's great black shed by the hard I found a fine new oyster smack being planked up. From the 1880s onwards old man Shuttlewood and later his son Frank had turned out many shapely smacks and a spritty barge or two, as well as a number of cruising yachts.

From here it was up the Crouch on the flood tide, through the crowded anchorage off Burnham, to Fambridge where there were at least twenty yachts of all sizes on moorings off the causeway. Here the ferryman rowed his black skiff across the river to South Fambridge when the bell tolled, for two-pence a head. In the manner of change, the last time I sailed through the anchorage at Fambridge some fifty years later, there were four lines of moorings for yachts stretching half a mile down river, and all of them modern glass-reinforced plastics types with the exception of two somewhat neglected-looking old stagers with gaff rigs.

These few glorious carefree days of sailing in and out of entirely new places were slipping past, and now, after I had anchored off Burnham for the last night, this strong wind had got up to plague an all-too-inexperienced young sailor. Admittedly, things had been going almost too well so far on this cruise, and there are times when it is perhaps as well that the fates decide to step in and let a man find himself dependent entirely on the elemental forces, unable to alter the conditions by pressing a switch or offering to pay money. There are indeed few things like a small boat without any mechanical power other than the sails and an oar to make a man feel at the mercy of the winds and the tides. It teaches him some respect for the elements, and he learns some humility.

In the circumstances, therefore, there seemed nothing to be done except indulge in the pleasant activity of sitting in the cockpit, while the gusts levelled the marram grass on the top of the bank, and just looking at all the yachts as they tugged at their moorings in the fairway. The dark red brick fronts and tiled roofs of the houses along the quayside were mellow and graceful, and I imagined had hardly changed the appearance of the waterfront for a hundred years. This was long before one of the local clubs, the Royal Corinthian, was to erect a flat roofed contemporary building of glass and concrete as its new clubhouse — a clever and no doubt highly suitable design for a club in some city perhaps, but in its setting at the end of the Burnham waterfront it appeared so brash and incongruous that I have since wondered how they could have brought themselves to do it.

There certainly were some very fine yachts in the anchorage, one or two old time yawls of 40 tons or so with square counters, a number of modern cutters with plenty of bow overhang (but still with bowsprits) and neat deckhouses, and numerous racing boats in various classes, for Burnham was the principal yacht racing port on the East Coast. But, as yet, not one of these yachts, nor any that I had seen at West Mersea, Maldon or elsewhere, was Bermudian rigged: that revolution in yachts' rigs was still to come.

On a mooring not far away, flanked by a handsome white steam yacht with a traditional fiddlehead bow and graceful counter stern and yellow funnel and two decidedly less elegant motor yachts with oversized deckhouses, lay a small black yawl of about 40ft or so with leeboards and her tanned mainsail brailed to the mast beneath a standing gaff. Her name, if memory plays none of its usual tricks, was *Boojum*. She represented a type of vessel of which I had already noticed several at West Mersea, two more on the mud off Heybridge, another at Maldon and three more at Paglesham — the small barge yacht.

Later I was to learn that the miniature barge had been introduced here on the Crouch by E B Tredwen in about 1892, and there were numbers of Tredwen-designed barge yachts in most yacht anchorages between the Medway and the Orwell. They were mostly without sheer and tended to look rather angular at the stern, and to some extent earned their nickname of 'flatirons' amongst the less sympathetic sailing men with elegant deep keel yachts of their own; but there were others from different builders which bore all the shapely features of the real spritty barges, even in some cases to carrying sprit rig.

Tredwen had the 10m *Pearl* built for his own use, and kept her for many years in this anchorage off the Corinthian. He not only used to sail her most weekends in winter as well as in summer, but cruised in her down Channel to the Cornish coast one summer, and as far as Berwick-on-Tweed and back to Burnham another year, showing that even a small barge could make coastal passages.

Looking back in retrospect I can call to mind quite a number of little barge yachts on the East Coast which ranged from some 14m in length down to 7m, and here are some: *Alceone, Billy Budd, Bird Alone, Chequers, Curlew, Dione, Doreen, Dormouse, Elizabeth Anne, Esna, Growler, Heron, Macara, Marietta, Mascotte, Nan, Nancy, Nancy Grey, Pearl, Peter Pan, Roonette, Seamew, Swan, Tiny Mite, Venus, Vera, Wavecrest*. Very few yachts of this barge type remain today, for they had many limitations, such as insufficient headroom, noise from the leeboards when at anchor, minimal space below the floorboards for bilge water or ballast, and a very jerky motion in a short sea. For their purpose of exploring shallow waters and sitting upright when aground they have been superseded by contemporary varieties of shallow draught, twin bilge keel yachts built in plywood or moulded in GRP.

The tide was well away now, for it had already fallen several feet on the stone facing of the river wall while I had been admiring all the yachts, and perhaps dreaming of the kind of boat I should love to have if I had the money. Suddenly it was borne in upon me that the sky appeared to be clearing a little and the wind was not quite so strong as it was. I had no barometer on board as I could not afford to buy one (the £36 cost of *Dabchick* and the pram dinghy had left very little of my share from the sale of the old cutter), and my suggestion at home that I might borrow for the week the handsome mercury barometer hanging like a banjo in the hall, which my father religiously tapped and sometimes swore at before leaving every morning, had been met with a lack of comprehension which I found almost hurtful. But on second thoughts it would have been a bit big for *Dabchick*'s cabin.

I could not tell, therefore, if the glass was rising or falling, but it did seem that the wind was drawing more down the river, more westerly, and the squalls were certainly scurrying across the anchorage with less violence. The thought that if I didn't go now and take the tide while it served we might never get back home in time, and that it could mean the sack from the office, drove me into action.

Dabchick responded to her reefed mainsail and small jib as though as willing to head for the home stables as any hack horse, and the pram followed on a rush of foam as we ran down to Shore Ends at the mouth of the Crouch with the ebb hurrying us along. It felt great to be underway again after only one forenoon at anchor and, as she wriggled and rolled her way over the swells, the mainboom one moment touching the water and the next pointing to the sky, the little boat seemed to revel in it. I found myself singing and shouting at the tiller, perhaps ignoring the signs that, far from easing off, this westerly wind was breezing up as fresh as ever, and the following seas were becoming just that bit steeper as we left the land astern. Not only that, but the sky was overcast again and a driving rain was drawing a grey blanket over the scene, blotting out the low shore Dengie way.

But the die was cast. Like a skier hurtling down the mountain slope, there could be no turning back now against this wind and tide: we had to go on. Certainly I had not bargained for this rain blotting out the scene, and as the minutes jogged by I tried to keep Messum's book from getting wet on the seat beside me while peering to leeward for a sight of the West Buxey buoy.

But the buoy was probably a mile away and invisible in this murk, and I fell to laying what appeared to be the correct compass course to leave the next mark, the Buxey beacon, to starboard. With the ebb more than half done, even with *Dabchick*'s modest one-metre draught I realized it would not do to miss our way through the narrow Rays'n channel, and I continued to search through the lee rigging for a sign of the beacon.

But no beacon appeared, while the seas became a little steeper and more sandy looking, and one angry little wave suddenly broke alongside and curled along the lee deck. Almost at the same instant I felt that sickening shock under me as the keel struck the sand. *Dabchick* rose on the next sea, surged onward, then as the swell raced ahead of her and her stern dropped, there was that shuddering bump again. Once more, lift, rush forward, then thud on the hard sand, almost jerking me off my feet.

The dinghy swung alongside to leeward on its painter and started hammering the rail as *Dabchick* came to a stop at last, heeled over to her deck. In desperation I hauled in the mainsheet to try to drive her off, but the wind only laid her over farther still and her bilge was being hammered on the ground. She was no longer moving ahead, but merely being struck by one angry little sea after another on her weather bilge, drenching me with spray.

Then I caught sight of the beacon through the rain, not where I had been looking for it, but to *port* of our course, the tall weed-covered post with its four ways topmark like a crossroads signpost gauntly mocking me. I now realized that I had not allowed for the way the ebb must set easterly across these sands as it poured out of the Crouch, and not straight down the Rays'n as I had assumed. It was a lesson to be remembered, but at the time a cruel one.

Any hope of hauling the boat off with the anchor was gone. We were much too far inside the beacon and the boathook showed that the sand was as level as a table all round. Disconsolately I clambered along the slanting cabin top and got the jib and mainsail down, and roughly stowed. Then aft again I crouched in the cockpit and waited while the shocks on her exposed hull grew less by degrees, and the boat finally settled over on her starboard bilge as though exhausted by the experience.

At last the waves ceased to shake her, and soon as if by magic the water had all drained away, leaving the sand in ripples almost dry. In seaboots I dropped overboard, the sand feeling as hard to the soles as any pavement, and walked towards the beacon carrying the anchor out as far as I could haul the chain. Then I returned aboard and tried to find some comfortable position on the lower settee to wait.

It would, I knew, be a long wait, at least five hours, before the tide would turn and the flood come back to float us off. It would be dark by then, and the savage beating of the halyards on the mast showed that there was no easing up of the wind as yet. To take my mind off the prospect of the seas that might be running across the sands when the tide made, I struggled to set the primus propped on a levelled locker lid, and brewed a cup of tea. It turned the rest of the cabin, slanting at an angle of fifty degrees or more, into a grotesque little world.

But the tea, with thick slices of bread and jam, put new heart into me, and I passed the hours contemplating the conventional shape of yachts in relation to the conditions in which so many of them — discounting the weekend round-the-buoys racers — sailed for most of their time. On this East Coast, I reflected, and probably in many other cruising grounds where sands and shoals abounded, there were miles and miles of sands offshore that lay bare at low water. All the rivers, too, had comparatively narrow navigable channels bounded by acres of mud banks, while some of the most attractive places a small craft could explore were the narrow winding creeks with very little depth of water in them. The Thames barges, I remembered, worked up these creeks to reach small quays where they discharged, or loaded, all kinds of cargoes like coal, slates, bricks, cement, timber, hay and agricultural produce — a hundred different commodities. And these barges were accordingly flat bottomed with very shallow draught, and surely, I reasoned, for the man who wants to cruise in such waters like the barges, there was much to be said for a yacht with a shallow draught and a strong hull that would not break up when caught on hard ground. The conventional yacht with her sharp bottom and deep keel when aground lay with her weakest part, the turn of the bilge, on the sand and stood a far greater chance of going to pieces before she could be floated off in a breeze.

The sun was shedding a fiery red glow through the clouds as it set behind the distant hills, and all too soon night began to darken the ridged sand all around. The wind continued its moaning notes through the yacht's rigging, but at least one consolation was that the rain had stopped. I was still anxious to know how my boat would fare before she lifted and floated off, for I was aware of a continuous sound in the air, a muffled roaring like that of a train passing over a very long girder bridge, but seemingly far away, and realized it was the seas breaking along the other edge of the sands as the tide made again.

On the Buxey with darkness coming on

The sound sent cold shivers down my spine, an intense feeling of loneliness swept over me, and I would have given anything to have had one of my chums with me now, just to have shared the situation and given moral support. For a moment I wondered whether I ought to light some kind of flare and call out help. But I didn't have any proper lifeboat flares — couldn't afford to buy them, even if I had thought about them before — and if I lit one of my precious blankets soaked in paraffin, I reasoned, who would see it out here on the Buxey and come to my rescue? The nearest place where there were boats was Brightlingsea, and that was many miles away.

No, I decided, feeling heroic for a moment, I had been careless enough to put my boat aground, and it was up to me to stick it out and get her off on the next tide, God willing. And if she did go to pieces before the tide floated her, like so many other vessels on these sands in the Thames Estuary — and I had to confess I had doubts just how sound she really was — did I not have a good, sturdy nine-foot pram dinghy in which it would be possible to row ashore on to the Dengie Flats?

At last the water was back, slopping all round the bilge and nudging the pram against the rail again. The first tremors showed that she was beginning to lift as the swells passed under her. Then as the water deepened they raised her a little further and let her drop back on to the sand with ever increasing shocks. It almost hurt me inside to feel my boat juddering like this, and to listen to the jingle of the cups and plates in the locker as they were bounced up and down. But at least, as I found by the light of a match in the cabin, she was not making any water, as yet.

By the time she was almost upright with her mast swinging in great arcs against the night sky, she was lifted bodily and dropped heavily on her keel, rattling all the rigging and loose gear below, over and over again. It felt murderous as it bounced me up and down in the cockpit, and I wondered how long this boat — any boat — could stand such treatment. I prayed for the tide to rise faster so as to get her afloat, but it seemed hours before she began to slew round, a little at a time, and then gradually the anchor chain came taut and she was no longer fleeting broadside across the sand.

Now was my chance. Whipping the reefed mainsail up with the sheet well payed off, I hauled in the chain bit by bit as she rose on each swell and thudded back on the sand again, inching her ahead against the wind and waves. Then at last the anchor was home and in its fairlead chock, the jib was run up and — heaven be praised — she heeled and was away on the port tack towards the deeper water of the Rays'n like a scalded cat. *Dabchick*, bless her stout heart, was free and sailing again!

The white flash of the friendly old Knoll buoy was just visible to the north to lead us fairly into the Wallet, and despite the weathergoing tide the seas here were not quite so steep as I had expected. But we now had the sands to wind-ward and as we ran slowly enough over the tide we had some shelter under their lee.

I was suddenly aware of a regular swishing sound in the cabin, and flinging open the doors was dismayed to find the floodboards well awash. The bumping had evidently strained her somewhere and she was making a lot of water. From then on I was compelled to divide my time between bailing with the bucket (for *Dabchick* had no fixed bilge pump) and short spells at the tiller, for the wind was on our starboard quarter and she could not be left for long on course.

For a time it seemed as if the water was gaining on me, and with the coast between Clacton and Walton within two miles or so to port I contemplated the necessity to ease her over that way and, if the worst came to the worst, let her run on to the beach. Once again I dearly wished one of my friends was with me to take the tiller while I bailed, for against the tide we were making only slow progress through sheering about so much.

Daylight was coming as high water came and went, and for a time the tide ran in our favour. I seemed to be keeping the water down in the cabin, but was thankful when I could gybe off the Naze and head up for Harwich Harbour. The ebb, of course, was now pouring out against us as I steered close round the end of Dovercourt breakwater into the calmer water of the harbour, but our progress over the ground had diminished to that of a snail. *Dabchick* was becoming more and more sluggish with the amount of water washing about inside her, and already it was soaking over the lee berth cushions. I knew I could not possibly keep on bailing and trying to sail her all the way up the Orwell to Ipswich — she would be more likely to sink on the way.

Over to port I could see that the beach looked steep close to Cann's shipyard, and on a sudden decision I headed the boat inshore until she grounded, and I was able to claw down the sails and make a rough stow. The tide soon left her lying over on her port side, and I was able to bail her out before getting round her and examining her bottom.

I soon found at least one place where she was obviously leaking, for a plank end was coming away from the sternpost. But how to mend it? I had not yet been able to accumulate any of those tools usually to be found aboard an old boat, such as caulking cotton and oakum, strips of canvas, pitch, copper sheeting for tingles, a hammer, galvanised nails and so on, and I should have to go into the town as soon as the shops opened and find something suitable.

A couple of unshaven characters appeared on the beach to ask why had I gone aground here with plenty of wa'er out there in the channel, and 'ow much was it worth to me for them to get a bo't and pluck me off. Happily before I could argue a third man of a better type came down and, looking carefully underneath the boat, asked 'Where did you buy this bo't?'

I told him, adding that I was told she was as sound as a bell, but hadn't been able to examine her much as she had been lying in a mud berth. He said 'Hm' non-committally and started testing some of the planking with a knife blade. 'She's got a few soft places around here,' he added, 'and one of the hood ends is sprung under the tuck. That's where the water's coming in. But don't worry, young mister, I'll get me tools and fix it for you'; and off he went.

He was soon back, and after testing some more of the planking with his knife, he worked in some soft stopping and caulking cotton and had the plank end nailed back in no time.

Before I could thank him he said 'That'll take you up to Ipswich all right, but if I was you I wouldn't go to *sea* in this bo't no more, I wouldn't. She's pretty ripe along them garboards.'

And with that he left, refusing to take anything more than the price of a drink, and when I tried to thank him he only laughed. 'Aw, it's nothing. We get a lot of jobs like this up at the yard,' and he nodded towards Cann's.

When the tide floated her off later in the day I sailed *Dabchick* back up the lovely Orwell to her mooring in the Bight, delighted to find she was making hardly any water, but hoping the boss wouldn't sack me in the morning for being a day late. To lose one's job in the 1920s could be a disaster.

One thing, however, stared me in the face. My faith in my boat was not as it had been, and her condition perhaps now explained why the man who sold her to me was pleased to throw in the new pram so cheaply. But I was already harbouring ideas of changing her for a little barge yacht, or at least a shallow centreboarder.

4

Nothing quite like a smack

Of all the yachting centres which have grown up in the area of the Thames Estuary since I started sailing, Pin Mill seems to have shown less change than any of them. The Butt and Oyster at the head of the hard was once extended to include a dining room, but is otherwise much as it was fifty years ago, both inside the bar and outside.

Behind the mellow roof of the pub the old shed in which Jack Powell used to cut the sails for smacks and barges, and for most of the local yachts, still stands, but it is much busier these days in the hands of the Ward family as a fascinating store for boat chandlery, yachting clothes and all the needs of the modern boatowner and his family. The cottages, smarter-looking than they used to be, have not been replaced by new development in the modern idiom. Any new building that has taken place has been mainly farther up the lane towards Chelmondiston village, where very little of the new development can be spotted from the anchorage.

The river hereabouts is now, of course, crowded with double lines of yacht moorings from a mile below the hard round Cathouse Point up to Woolverstone and the small marina near the Royal Harwich clubhouse, almost two miles of yachts of all kinds on both sides of the river. Generations of yachtsmen have been coming to Pin Mill, for it has always been one of the prettiest anchorages anywhere on the east coast of England.

Not many years back Frank Perkins, who in the early 1930s founded the now giant Perkins diesel engine factory at Peterborough, had an 11m bilge keel sloop which he called

Little Claudia built to one of my designs and decided to keep her at Pin Mill when he retired as he had many happy memories of the place from his early sailing days. 'Until I brought my boat here,' he told me one day on the hard, 'I hadn't visited Pin Mill since the summer of 1910 when I sailed here last. And that's over fifty years ago, and do you know, it looks much the same to me as it did then.'

My own earliest recollections of the anchorage were from trips made to Harwich and Felixstowe and back when taken by my parents on one of the paddle steamers run by the Great Eastern Railway. There were then three of these small vessels, *Norfolk*, *Suffolk* and *Essex*, which started their regular summer trips from the New Cut at Ipswich. The electric tram would turn off Wherstead Road and deposit you and the other passengers at the foot of Bath Street close to the steamer landing, and what excitement it was for a small boy to run ahead and see which boat was to be 'ours' today.

All three paddlers were double-ended, having a sharp bow with a rudder incorporated at each end, so that they had no need to turn either in the Cut or on their triangular course between Harwich Ha'penny Pier and Felixstowe dock. Their masts and black and buff funnels (*Norfolk* had one amidships, the others two) accordingly had no rake whatever, and over the white paddleboxes the side light boards were in pairs, back to back, one red the other green. I never did know which was officially port and which starboard.

It was a wonderful way to go to Pin Mill, instead of by road in one of the boneshaking motorbuses with their solid tyres, for if you remembered to warn the captain in good time he would give a long pull on the whistle as the steamer rounded the Inkpot buoy off Cathouse. Harry Ward (grandfather of the present Jack Ward) would then row out from the hard in his skiff, always facing forward, and with paddlewheels stopped you were handed on to the sponson by one of the crew and dropped down into Harry's boat. Then while he rowed you to the hard, or aboard your own boat, the steamer went on her way laying a wide carpet like gingerbeer froth in her wake, and your young chest swelled with importance. Pin Mill in its beautiful setting seemed a heavenly anchorage just then.

The *Essex* was sold out of this service just before the 1914 War, and the *Norfolk* and *Suffolk* returned after war service for only a few more years on the Orwell. With the grouping of all the country's railways into four great systems at the end of 1922, the Great Eastern lost its sixty years of independence and found itself part of the vast London and North Eastern Group. Change and reorganisation were in the air, and within a few years these delightful river trips by steamer were withdrawn for good.

It was not only Pin Mill that offered attraction for the day tripper (or the sailing man), for Harwich Harbour, like a minor Portsmouth, was still a very active naval port. There were always grey ships of various classes at anchor, and steam picket boats foaming past with impressive smoke trails, to draw passengers to the rail with cries of 'Coo, look at that!' And until the shore establishment with its famous mast was completed on Shotley Point, the naval school was based in HMS *Shotley II* which rode to moorings in the Stour off the jetty.

I recall this vessel as a big, handsome, three-masted ship-rigged steam vessel painted in the brave style of pre-battleship grey days, with black hull, white lining above a red boot top, white upperworks and two short, yellow ochre funnels. Launched in 1865, she was originally HMS *Minotaur*, and with a length of 122m was one of the longest single screw iron-clads in the Navy. For many years until the 1950s, I believe, her five-masted near-sistership, *Agincourt* of 1863, was moored in the entrance to the Medway doing duty as a coal hulk, and beneath the gaunt cranes on deck and the general layer of coaldust you could discern as you sailed past the hand-some hull and figurehead and fine lines of this splendid old warrior of ironclad days.

The premises of the Royal Harwich Yacht Club, before they were moved to Woolverstone, were across the harbour and commanded a fine view of the starting line, so that steamer passengers could see all that was going on on race days. It was then the custom for yachts of what was known as the Big Class to commence their racing season with the RHYC regatta. The presence of His Majesty's cutter *Britannia* always drew every kind of vessel to watch.

What a sight those great racing cutters were as they jilled around by the starting line, their every movement carried out, as it were, in slow motion. There was no flipping about from one tack to another in the manner to today's finkeel racers: they went about in stays with the grace of a tall woman dancing a stately pavane; and while they were head to wind and the crews moved to their new stations on deck, the wind ran in slow undulations across the white canvas of their enormous mainsails. There was nothing like the frenzied fluttering of today's strips of mainsail.

But these great cutters were indeed larger than life, with their large crews and their days already numbered. *Lulworth, White Heather, Terpsichore* and Lipton's green-hulled *Shamrock V* were known as '23-Metres' and were in the 150 to 175 tons TM bracket, while the beautiful black *Britannia*, the King's own yacht, measured 212 tons TM. No wonder they seemed to do nothing in a hurry.

These big yachts were all gaff cutter rigged with bowsprits, and had mainbooms reaching well out beyond the long counter sterns, so that when it breezed up the whiteclad hands (crew members to the modern yachtsman) shinned out on the boom so as to reach the leech tackle for tucking in a reef. But for me perhaps the most impressive sight was *Britannia*'s huge jackyard topsail, its canvas setting as smooth as a sheet of white paper without a wrinkle anywhere, together with the tiny figure of the hand whose job it was to climb aloft and make fast the downhaul.

If memory serves, it was at the regatta the following season, in 1923, that the beautiful 23-Metre *Nyria*, owned by Mrs R E Workman, first astonished everyone by appearing with an immensely tall Marconi mast and a great jibheaded mainsail. There was much speculation as to how she would perform with that lofty spar, and she seemed at first to play into the hands of the critics by proving fractionally slower than her rivals on a broad reach and when on a dead run. When they came on the wind close-hauled, however, she showed such marked superiority, being so much closer winded, that in a few seasons first one and then the others of the Big Class were converted to the Marconi rig, later to be misnamed the Bermudian.

When *Britannia* herself reappeared from Camper and Nicholsons' yard with the lofty mast and the new rig she immediately lost much of the character she had displayed ever since G L Watson had designed her for Edward, then Prince of Wales, in 1893. Much of the eye-catching beauty of the Big Class, as well as most of the racing classes that followed the new trend, disappeared for ever when these yachts lost their individual jackyard cutter rigs, and appeared as uniform triangles of white on the horizon. But the new Bermudian undoubtedly improved their racing performance, it was easier to handle with less gear, and the number of hands on deck could be reduced from about twenty to fifteen or so. There would be no point in turning the clock back solely in favour of the beauty of gaff rig and flowing sails.

My private regret since seeing these yachts race off Harwich has been that I never managed to visit Cowes in time to see the irascible South African T B Davis's great schooner *Westward* racing. Compared with even the largest of today's offshore racers she was impressive — 323 tons TM — with a row of portholes along her side, and only in Beken's photographs of her storming up the Solent in a breeze of wind with *Britannia* and others of the class can you get some idea of the sport of kings which was never to be seen again. Yet, following these thoughts even further back, to a Cowes week a year or two before the start of the First World War, what an event that must have been when the Kaiser's great schooner, *Meteor III*, bigger than Davis' *Westward*, racing in a gale force squall, lay over suddenly out of control and went foaming away to leeward with her long bowsprit pointing at one of the other yachts in the race. While the overpressed schooner hurled to the winds all the theories about centres of effort and lateral resistance, metacentric height and the balance of forces, the men at the wheel fought to get her to luff. But for timeless moments, it seemed, she refused to obey the helm, while the horrified crew crouched helpless as the sheets were belayed by the lee rail, and that was several feet beneath rushing water. Happily *Meteor* began to come round under control once more just before she rammed the racing cutter to leeward. But what a sight that must have been in the tumbling green waters of the Solent!

45

After *Dabchick* had been sold and was sailed away by her owners to their own mooring on the Lower Thames, I began to search all places where boats were to be found within a day's ride on my bike, hoping to come across a small barge yacht within my very limited price. At one place there was just such a boat that greatly took my fancy, a beautifully kept barge yacht, but the owner wouldn't part with her, and I began to despair of finding anything like what I had in mind. At my figure there seemed to be only very old straight stemmed cutters with deep keels, or hideously converted lifeboats.

There were countless scores of these conversions scattered around the coasts in those days, for they enabled the poor man to build himself a yacht by degrees. Because of the existing Board of Trade rule that all the boats on ships of British registry must be replaced every so often regardless of condition, there was naturally a constant supply of these clinker-built, double-ended boats in sizes ranging from 18ft (5.5m) up to 30ft (9.1m) in length. Some had hardly ever been off the ship's davits and were in first rate condition available for £30 to £40 or so; others needing some repairs might be had for a few pounds.

This source of cheap hulls has since then almost dried up, for ships' boats are now mass produced in steel, light alloy or in moulded fibreglass, and their life in davits, even on tropical runs, is many times longer and they are accordingly not discarded in such numbers. Besides, there are now not so many very poor boating men with only a few pounds to spare; most can afford to buy a second-hand boat outright, while there are now yacht purchase finance companies ready to help you get a boat that you can't possibly afford to buy yet.

How I found the 24ft (7.3m) centreboarder *Wild Lone* and cruised around the Estuary in her for a season, and eventually bought *Swan*, the smart little barge yacht I had already seen and coveted, has been told elsewhere* and need not be repeated here. Let it suffice to say that a death in the family and break up of the home resulted in my choosing to try to make a living as a freelance journalist in London. For two miserable years with little prospect, therefore, there was no sailing, until a little book I had written, *Yachting on a Small Income*, led me by devious means to being asked to edit a

Swatchways and Little Ships

newly launched fortnightly yachting paper. And a year later this resulted in my appointment in a similar capacity to the *Yachting Monthly* magazine.

It was early the following year, in January, that I was offered the chance of a good sail. A friend had recently bought a converted Colchester smack lying in Heybridge Basin, and wanted to get her round to Fambridge as soon as possible so as to complete fitting-out at his own berth there, and asked whether I would care to help him round with her the next weekend. It seemed a heaven-sent release from the cold rain and fogs of London, and I jumped at it.

There was no taxi at the station when our train pulled into Maldon East on the Friday evening, but we had only our kit-bags and gumboots to carry and were already used to the mile and a half walk along the canal to the Basin. The canal was then lined with willows on both banks, and with regular horse-drawn barge traffic to and from Chelmsford the towpath was good for walking. Today no timber barges pass along the waterway and the path is completely overgrown.

Our stores were waiting for us at Mrs Borer's shop by the lock. It was necessary only to post a day or two before a list of what was wanted — bread, eggs, butter, meat, sausages, tin stuffs, matches, paraffin, or whatever — and the box containing them would be ready to ship aboard when you arrived. The little store is now a private house, but the helpful service rendered to more than one generation of yachtsmen at the Basin is commemorated in its present name — Borer's House.

The grey and black hull of David's smack was lying close to the lock, and we soon had the bogie stove roaring and our blankets airing as the cabin warmed up. She was a fine ship about 35ft (10.7m) in length with something over 10ft (3.1m) beam and had the typical square counter and lengthy bowsprit of the Colchester oyster smacks. David had mentioned that his ship had never had an engine, and although it was cold enough to lay a coating of hoar frost over the decks, I was glad the breeze was holding in the north, for it would help us through the lock and give us a fair wind for the Crouch.

The sky was clear and the stars looked bright as diamonds as their reflections rocked lazily on the still water of the canal. While my skipper stowed the provisions below I felt my way round the deck so as to get familiar with the layout of the sheets and halyards. Having satisfied myself that I knew where essentials were I lost no time sniffing the keen night air, but dropped down into the warmth below and closed the hatch after me. From forward came a cheerful sizzling above the roar of a primus.

'No place when it's cold like a boat's cabin, is there?' David's cheerful face was momentarily framed in the doorway to the fo'c's'le, revealing all the happiness of a proud new owner. 'How many sausages can you eat, MG?'

He was a good skipper and I felt that I should be able to learn a lot from watching him this weekend, for David had been sailing around the East Coast many more years than I had, often single-handed in the various boats he himself had owned, and like the experienced single-handed sailing man he had his own way of doing things and preferred not to ask his crew to do them.

We had been tempted to go out on the night's tide, but he wisely decided that as we were unfamiliar with the ship's gear in the dark, and in any case had a good deal to attend to to get her ready for the passage, it would be wiser — and certainly warmer — to stay in the Basin and lock out on the 0900 tide next morning. We were able to relax, therefore, and enjoy the warmth of the fire and soft lamplight in the euphoria that follows a long and active day and a good meal.

Daylight brought grey skies and a little more wind, but still in the north and ideal for our course to the Crouch. While my skipper went along to the lock keeper's cottage to warn him that we wanted to get out as soon as possible, I unfrapped the halyards, bent on the jib and fore staysail, and loosened the mainsail tiers for quick hoisting. The yachts lining the bank of the canal for a quarter of a mile or more looked deserted and forlorn under their winter covers, their masts devoid of running gear. It was evidently too cold and wintry this week-end for their owners to make a start on the fitting-out so early in the year, and ours was the only boat casting off warps.

Even at this early hour Mrs Borer was at the door of her shop to give us a cheery wave. 'Hope you make a good passage,' she called out. 'It's a fair wind for you, isn't it?' It was just high water when Jack Ellis, the lock master, opened the outer gates and with staysail only set we nosed out into the river. 'See you've got your stove a going,' he grinned. 'You'll need it!'

The dinghy — the smack's skiff — lay secured bottom up against the starboard rail, and the old girl began to slip through the water making hardly a sound as I swigged up the peak halyards and set the jib. Although the wind was only light it felt icy as we stamped our feet on the deck and beat numbed fingers to bring back some circulation. David stood with his back to the wind and his rump against the curved tiller, for as with most smacks there was no cockpit, only a low square hatch leading down to the lazarette.

Osea Island slid by to port, the first of the ebb running through the rotting posts of the little pier. The old Barnacle still stood like a black sentinel thinking of the days of the great *Jullanar*, and then we were slipping past the Stone to starboard with its new bungalows and chalets. The ebb was carrying us down handsomely.

'No use our trying to run up through the Rays'n', said David as if voicing my own thoughts. 'It would be too late on the tide for our draught. What do you think we should do, MG, have a bit of a sail round Bench Head and put into Mersea Quarters for the night, or,' he paused, stooping to look under the mainsail to leeward, 'or carry on and go through the Wallet Spitway?'

I had no hesitation in voting for the Spitway, where I knew there would be more water. 'We should be inside Shore Ends well before dusk,' I added, 'and bring up inside the Crouch somewhere for the night. You never know what tomorrow might be like'.

My skipper nodded his approval. 'Like to take her while I get the old pipe going?'

It felt great to stand leaning back against the tiller, collar turned up, woollen cap pressed well down over the ears, hands keeping warm in pockets, and to feel this sturdy smack surging through the swells. Like most old-fashioned craft with a long straight keel she kept herself steadily on course with hardly any movement of the helm, and the confidence she gave in her ability to deal with any of the seas without bouncing wildly up and down warmed the heart.

While below, David was not only lighting his pipe but

stoking up the stove, for a trail of smoke and sparks began to dip under the mainsail and blow away to leeward like a grey cloud. His face appeared in the hatchway and he handed out a steaming mug of coffee. 'Br-rr,' he exclaimed glancing up to windward, 'Looks like snow in that sky. Have you sighted the Spitway buoy yet?'

The spherical bell and light buoy passed close to port as we bore away and gybed her over for the short run through the narrow channel between the Buxey and the Gunfleet sands, and pointed our bowsprit a little to windward of the Swin Spitway buoy to allow for the set of the tide. David came on deck, picked up the leadline, and with the deftness born of practice took two quick casts, keeping a light hold on the line through his hands so that at no time did it go slack.

'Fathom and a quarter,' he remarked as he flaked the line down on deck again. 'Enough for our five-foot draught with hardly any sea to speak of. But I reckon that barge will be cutting it a bit fine, won't she?' and he nodded at a spritty coming down Swin a mile or so away with a fine bone at her bluff bows, evidently heading for the Spitway.

As she passed to leeward we exchanged a wave with her skipper at the wheel. 'She's deep laden and must be drawing seven foot under her leeward chine. But then,' David added with a smile, 'I guess she's been this way many times before, and her skipper knows the way!'

In the Swin ourselves now, I hauled in the mainsheet while my skipper attended to the jib and foresheets, and the smack started to nose into the short swells with the wind a little forward of our starboard beam. It was still a little shy and although we were making we reckoned four and half knots through the water, the tide that had been giving us an additional knot and a half down from the Blackwater was now running against us, and taking a knot and a half away: in short, halving our speed over the ground from six knots to three. At this rate the gaunt post of the Whitaker beacon with its topmark like a half-opened umbrella seemed to be passing to leeward with great reluctance, as though sorry to see us go by.

All things come, so it is said, to him who waits, and as the afternoon drew on, the buoy marking the Sunken Buxey —

shown on the charts in those days as the West Buxey —
dragged itself past with the tide sucking lazily around its sides,
and the low line of the sea wall at Shore Ends began to detach
itself from the grey water off the bowsprit end. From out of
the slate grey sky to windward the first flurries of snow began
to blow round us, for the moment blotting out the land ahead
and finding weak points in our clothing.

It was too cold standing on deck to have long spells at the
tiller, and we took it in turns to drop below into the cabin
which was as warm as a ship's boiler room, to thaw out and to
hand a mug of soup to the helmsman. Darkness was closing in
early as the snow increased in earnest, silently covering the
decks in white, the flakes settling in the mainsail with a muted
whisper.

We were inside the river now and could see the bank on
the weather side white already against the dark sky. It all
seemed silent and eerie as we continued to sail up slowly into a
blank wall of snowflakes ahead.

'No point in trying to get any further before it's dark',
David remarked. 'We'll edge a bit closer to the north shore
and let go for the night. Hand the stays'l, will you, MG, and
then toppinglift and trice up the main tack.'

The smack rounded up towards the bank while I muzzled
the jib, being showered with light snow as it flogged in the
wind. As the smack lost all forward way David clumped
forward and let the anchor go with a heavy splash. Then he
payed-out the rusty cable over the windlass barrel as the
smack began to drop astern and snubbed on the chain, giving
the anchor a satisfying snub to bite well into the ground. He
was too wise an old bird to make the common mistake of
dropping the anchor too soon, while the yacht is still shooting
ahead, and thereby risking drawing a bight of the cable round
the anchor when she dropped astern. An anchor inside a loop
of its own chain is almost bound to drag when a strain comes
on it.

While this wind held in the north we should be as safe and
snug as anywhere on the coast, and when the riding light had
been hoisted on the forestay and the cabin hatch closed, we
settled to a yarn and a good meal of stew and dumplings,
potatoes and sprouts, and tinned fruit and coffee, with David's

trusty pipe to follow. For myself I was content to do the washing up, for I had given up smoking for the next few years.

As we wrenched ourselves from our warm blankets next morning and looked out of the hatch, we were met with a world covered in white. Every part of the smack had a coating of two or three inches of snow, except where the deck was bare in a circle round the base of the stove chimney. It was snowing heavily and the river bank could be seen only dimly to windward.

'High water in just two hours,' said my skipper. 'Quick brekka first, then we'll get underway and make Fambridge easily on the tide.'

With eggs and bacon and coffee inside us, we levered in some of the cable with the windlass, soon getting into the swing of inserting the handspikes in the holes in the barrel and hauling them round. Then with mainsail set we paused on the foredeck until the smack took a slow sheer to port and the boom wavered and shook over the lee quarter; David broke out the anchor while I hoisted the jib, and nipped aft to sheet it home. And the knowing old hooker, having carried out this routine manoeuvre thousands of times in her forty years, stood bravely up river on the tide, with nobody fussing her at the helm. That is, for me, one of the joys of working a smack or any well-balanced old-time yacht: the way the boat seems to know what is wanted of her, like a well-trained sheep dog.

Burnham anchorage looked bleak and utterly deserted as we sailed through it. There was not a single yacht afloat, for they were all on legs along the foreshore or tucked away inside sheds for the winter. Even the familiar waterfront with its mellow buildings appeared washed of all colour today under the blanket of white. Not a soul could be seen on the quay: the place looked like a mediaeval town of the dead, and was soon lost in the curtain of snow astern.

The breeze was fairly steady and allowed us, hardening in the sheets that felt crisp and stiff as rods in the hands, to lay up Cliff reach without making a tack. As the dreary banks slid past on either side, visible only dimly through the snow, and our sails became white boards against the dark sky, we warmed our hands on hog mugs of something nourishing and sang in the icy air with the satisfaction of having made such a trouble-free passage.

As we came up to the anchorage off Fambridge I could see two rather forlorn unrigged yachts still afloat, and one or two black mooring buoys riding the tide in the channel.

'That's my mooring over the bowsprit end,' said David, pointing. 'If you'll stow the jib, MG, I'll scandalize the mains'l, and round her up.'

In a long slow sweep, with the jib hastily lashed to the bowsprit and the mainsail with tack triced up almost to the gaff jaws, and the peak halyards eased away until the gaff hung just below the horizontal, so that all wind was spilled from the canvas, the old smack forged methodically up to the mooring buoy, and David had it aboard with a deft lift of the boathook.

A small figure on the bank near the big black shed was giving a wave. David waved back.

'That's Mr Flick who looks after our boats,' he explained. 'Nice of him to turn out to welcome us.'

It was indeed warming to think our lonely arrival in the anchorage had not gone unnoticed, and David had brought his new purchase home in fine style.

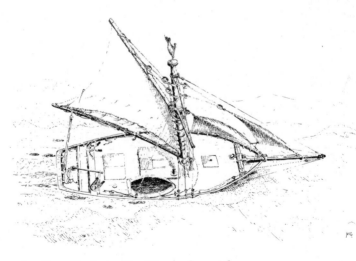

A gull could admire David's sturdy smack

5

Trouble on the bar

Beneath an overcast sky an early evening was laying a slight mist over the saltings on the other side of the river. Little by little the tide was creeping stealthily over the mud, searching with wet fingers into all the shallow pools and gullies, where tiny crabs menaced each other with outstretched claws and wary beady eyes.

From over the river wall the sound of Maldon's church clock came musically on the gentle breeze. Seven o'clock. We ought soon to be afloat, for the incoming tide was already feeling its way round the yacht's bilge as she loomed almost upright in the mud. My shipmate's ruddy face, crowned jauntily with a knitted woollen bobcap, emerged from the cabin with the washup bowl in his hand bringing with him a savoury smell from the galley.

'Suppose it's all right,' he asked quietly, 'to ditch the potato peelings here?'

I said of course, wondering at his concern for I didn't own this anchorage, little imagining that within a few years anti-pollution campaigns would be invented. That was one of the things I liked about Duncan: his thoughtfulness when aboard another's boat. He was always a welcome shipmate, for he was hefty and as strong as a horse — a useful attribute aboard a nine-tonner whose only mechanical power was an ash sweep — and he shared with me an infectious enthusiasm for cruising in small boats. He was twenty years my senior, and had already been my skipper when I had sailed in one or other of his boats; for like me he tended to change his own craft every few years.

It was nine or ten years, I recalled, since as a greenhorn I had crewed him several weekends in his old Nore One Design centreboarder *Albatross,* and on one occasion we had come near to losing her (as well as ourselves) on the Gunfleet sands, as has been told elsewhere★. While we had each gained since then, I suppose, experience in our different ways, Duncan was the best kind of mate a fellow could wish for, for when crewing for anyone else he accepted the skipper's decisions and never became argumentative. He was a bank official, and when years later he retired he refuted the accepted dictum that the average bank manager's expectation of life after retirement was but two years by continuing to draw his pension for another thirty-five years! When he died in his nineties it was spring, and he was even then looking forward to getting his last boat, a small motor cruiser, afloat for the season.

But all this was in the future as he and I sat waiting for *Nightfall* to float on the tide. Duncan had agreed to join me for this weekend early in April with the vowed intention of sailing her round to Aldeburgh where I had friends who wanted to see my new boat. We had travelled together in the train from Liverpool Street on what were known as yachtsmen's weekend tickets. These were a welcome facility for sailing men who spent weekends sailing from one place to another round the coast, as they enabled one to return from a different station free, or on paying a mileage excess if the port of return was farther than the departure point. It was a relic of Great Eastern days made as a concession through the applications of the Cruising Association, and that first season with *Nightfall* I made full use of the facility, sailing her up and down the coast each weekend the wind and tides were right between the Crouch and Lowestoft.

Our train had been delayed on the Maldon branch, and by the time D and I arrived on the river wall by the Blackwater Sailing Club, my boat had just taken the ground as the tide ebbed, and we had to hurry out in the dinghy before she dried out in the soft mud.

'Never mind, old chap,' said my cheerful shipmate as we stowed our gear. 'I never tire of just looking at this place, it's always so peaceful. And I like to think of what it must have looked like when the Danes invaded these parts in their long-

★*Magic of the Swatchways*

ships, and were beaten by the Saxons defending the old town of Maldon — or was it the other way about: the Saxons were defeated and the Vikings overran the place? Didn't the battle happen about here, on the causeway between the mainland and Northey island over there?'

I had to confess my knowledge of history in these waters before the Norman Invasion was just as sketchy as my friend's but it was pleasant to think that the scenery hereabouts must have changed little since those stirring days. *Nightfall*, however, was drawing attention to herself by stirring gently, then fleeting on her keel inch by inch until she was tugging on her mooring chain, afloat again. By this time the excellent meal D had cooked had been eaten and cleared away, and we had decided on principle to get underway if the light south-westerly breeze held, and to run down the river for the rest of the night.

With her tanned mainsail and large jib set *Nightfall* made steadily over the tide, for these were the lazy friendly neap tides that may not be such urgent friends as spring tides but are not such implacable enemies when they ran foul. Darkness was soon with us and the mist that had almost hidden the saltings was blowing lazily past us like wraiths in a dream, and it was only by cautious steering by the oil-lit compass that we were able to find our way down past the channel buoys — the two Doubles, the Doctor and *Dirk*'s mooring off Osea Pier — and so into the main part of the wide river.

Nightfall and her habits were as yet somewhat new to me. I had found this 9.5m gaff sloop during the winter in a boat shed in Norfolk, for she had been built for a private owner for Broads cruising back in 1910. She was unlike the local hire boats, however, in having a long straight keel from the fore-foot to the rudder heel, and she must have been awkward in stays when turning up any of the narrower rivers. She had had an auxiliary motor, a vintage two-stroke Boulton and Paul of six horsepower, but on the trip round from Lowestoft before a fresh easterly wind I had carelessly allowed the cylinder to become flooded through the straight exhaust pipe. The engine became seized solid and never turned again, and I had to have it taken out. For this season, at least, I had decided to sail without any engine, for *Nightfall* proved a very handy boat and easy enough to move with her sweep when necessary. Except for one metre which I had had cut off the mainboom so that it only just reached the counter, she was sloop rigged as originally designed for the Broads, with a fair sized jib on a 1½-metre bowsprit. This weekend with Duncan was to change that.

'I don't know about you, old man,' said the black, oil-skinned figure at the helm, 'but we've passed Bradwell, the wind seems to be dying, and it's getting mighty cold, as well as rather late. . . .'

D's hint was all I needed to make up my mind. We had made a good start considering how light the wind was, and now it had come on to rain, a few drops pattering on the cabin top at first, but then a persistent gentle downpour. It seemed senseless carrying on into the darkness ahead, even though we now had the ebb with us. We would make the passage into the Orford river in the morning.

'Good idea, D,' I said, 'if you'll luff up towards the shore we'll bring up close in to Sales Point here, and get a few hours good sleep. I'll take a cast or two.'

With the jib rolled up on the Wykeham Martin furling gear, D steered *Nightfall* breasting the tide under her mainsail alone towards the almost invisible shore, while I dropped the lead a few times.

'Three fathoms. That'll do us nicely.'

While my shipmate rounded her up into the wind I quickly braced up the topping lift, lowered the mainsail and slipped a couple of tiers loosely round the gaff and boom. As soon as she had lost all forward way the anchor was dropped and the cable payed out until it brought up at ten fathoms mark with a satisfying snub, in accordance, I recalled with a chuckle, with David and his smack's teaching. Although this was only a neap tide the ebb here was soon flowing past the taut chain with a merry little trickle. Meanwhile D had got the riding light ready to hoist on the forestay while I made a better stow of the mainsail. When at anchor we did not set up those unwieldy scissors boom crutches, a relic of Broadland practice, as a taut topping lift and mainsheet kept the boom thoroughly quiet.

To the yachtsman of long experience the routine of

bringing up to a mooring or anchor, and of getting underway, has become almost second nature, and its sequences are taken for granted, their description seemingly trivial. Yet to the newcomer it seems anything but simple, and it is all too easy to get his little ship into a mess, so that he has to learn how to cope with varying conditions either through the sound tuition of an instructor or through the hard school of trial and error. What, for instance, we all take for granted, namely the ease with which we walk, is one of the most difficult exercises that a baby has to learn. There is nothing simple about it, and it usually takes a small child a long time to master foot control and balance and stance. Similarly learning to speak one's language is a slow and often painful process, and one which does not come naturally to a child's mouth. So with the infinite tactics of handling small vessels in a tideway.

'Come on, skipper! It's a lovely morning, and there's a nice breeze from sou'west.' D's voice sounded positively boisterous, and I could hear his feet on deck. 'What about a dip, eh?'

His insistence could not be ignored for long, and after a feeble attempt I dragged myself out of the warm sleeping bag and sniffed the chilly air with only my head out of the hatch. Somehow the thought of a plunge overboard at that early hour made me wince, and assuring him that I would try to resist the temptation by attending to breakfast for him, I dropped below again and started the primus. Somehow the smell of frying eggs and bacon and coffee must have wafted out through the open hatch, for I heard no heavy 'k'flump' as my friend dived overboard, and he shortly appeared still in pyjamas and as dry as a bone. 'I thought it might delay breakfast if I had a swim,' he explained, and pretended to look hurt when I laughed.

Nightfall was underway an hour before high water, running before a smart south-westerly with the short following seas glinting in the sunshine. The rain of the previous night had gone, and the scene wore that fresh, rain-washed look of a bright April morning. As the end of the land at Sales Point drew past we talked of the lonely building that stands close to the river wall, and how it came to be there. On that site had been an extensive Roman fort, called Othona, which guarded the entrance to the Blackwater with a smaller complementary fortification on Mersea Island opposite. This river and the Colne running up to Colchester played an important part for Roman shipping as well as the cultivation of oysters. For Colchester (then Camulodunum) was the principal centre for Roman activities in Essex as good roads led from the city to all East Anglian places from London to the Wash.

After the Romans left Britain to its own devices and barbarism set in for some centuries Christianity began to filter through the country little by little. The site of Othona was selected to spread the gospel and a Saxon preacher, Bishop Cedd, was empowered to build a chapel on the Essex shore for the purpose. He chose the site of the ruined fortification because it already had its own quay onto what is now Ray Sand Channel, and there was an abundance of bricks, stones and rubble to hand from the surrounding walls of the fort. Completed about 660 AD, it still stands, now lovingly restored, and services are regularly held during the summer months.

At this state of tide there would be ample water over Colne Bar, and I accordingly steered *Nightfall* between the black bar buoy with its ball topmark and the end of the land. Away to port in the vicinity of the white Fishery buoy a smart, grey-painted gaff sloop with tanned sails was riding hove-to with foresail a-weather, rising and falling regularly over the short seas.

'Isn't that one of the Colne police boats?' D remarked. 'Nice job for a bobby on the beat, I'd say, if he likes sailing!'

It certainly did look an enviable life for a keen young sailing fiend, I agreed, but perhaps not quite so heavenly in autumn fogs — when the would-be poacher sailed his smack inside the limits hidden in the fog — nor during the months of winter snow and gales; for the patrol had to go on night and day. And an eight hour spell of duty just jilling around a few square miles of water, hove-to part of the time as this boat was, we both admitted, would surely pall on the keenest sailor.

There were then, I believe, five of these sloops in the Colne Police Fishery service, trim little gaff sloops 7 to 8 metres in length, *Alexandria, Colne, Prince of Wales, Raven* and *Victoria,* and they were normally manned by a policeman in uniform with peaked cap. A launch put out from Brightlingsea at the end of each spell of duty with the man's relief, and the changeover was always made smartly between launch and sloop while both were underway. So far as I know none of these little boats while in the service ever had an engine fitted, but after the Hitler war they were replaced by noisy motor boats.

'We're making good time now we've got the ebb under us,' D beamed as he hugged the tiller. 'Look how Walton pier is coming up on us.'

It was an exhilarating run, and over the Stone Banks off Harwich the seas were a little steeper, and our dinghy started to run up on us before some of the more boisterous ones. But we had by now learnt how to cope with this bad habit of towed dinghies, and always made it a rule when starting on a coastal passage (always, did I say? Well, when I remembered in time) to shackle two painters on to the dinghy's eyebolt at the foot of its stem. We now cast off one of these to trail astern as a drogue, and veered the stouter one to about six fathoms. This arrangement, we had found, was more effective in braking the dinghy's wild rush down the face of a following sea, as it allowed its stern to slew to one side or the other if it wanted to. If the drogueline is towed from the stern it is less effective as it keeps the dinghy's transom square on to the seas. Moreover, when no longer running before it, it is much easier to retrieve the drogue painter from the dinghy's stem than from its transom, while the yacht is still sailing at all fast.

The breeze was steadily piping up as the white cottages at Shinglestreet came into view through the lee shrouds, and *Nightfall* was beginning to run a little wild as D wrestled with the helm. Ahead of us we could just make out the small black buoy that marked the Orford Haven entrance, appearing only every now and then as its topmark showed above the seas.

'Another roll or two in the main, do you think, skipper?' suggested the mate. 'She's getting a bit hard to hold.'

But I shook my head. Truth to tell I was feeling all the pride of the new owner in the way his ship was behaving, running like a startled deer, even if she was becoming a little wild, with the wave on each side of the bow a cushion of hissing foam rolling over to fall astern and rise again alongside the cockpit in a rail wetting quarter wave. She really was going about as fast as she could, and it seemed to me a pity to shorten her down now when we were so near to the mouth of the river.

'Hardly worth putting a reef in now, D,' I said. 'We'll be over the bar soon, and with the tide dropping all the time I don't want to run it too close, you know. This is a nasty bar anywhere near low water.'

The words were hardly out of my mouth when there was a bang like a pistol shot, the lee rigging went slack, and the mast bent forward like a fishing rod.

'My God, the weather shroud's gone!'

Commendably calm, D pushed the helm down smartly and brought the yacht round to starboard in a wild sweep.

'Mainsheet! We must get her on to the other tack.'

Good boat that she was, *Nightfall* didn't lose way while I quickly overhauled the sheet but came up into the wind, hovered for a moment on a breaking sea, then payed off on to the port tack with the jibsheet a-weather. D pushed the helm down again and put the slipline on it, and *Nightfall* calmed herself and settled quietly, lying hove-to and rising and falling methodically over the seas as we had seen the Colne police boat doing.

D was already at the mast, catching the loose shroud as it swung away to leeward. 'Rigging screw's parted,' he called back. 'Got a spanner, oh, and some hambro line, skipper?'

Together we removed the two parts of the broken bottle screw from the eye of the shroud and the chain plate, then set to with a length of stout hambro line to make lanyards, seizing the two eyes and setting them up in old-fashioned traditional style. While I finished off the ends, my excellent shipmate wound up four rolls in the mainboom, and in less than ten minutes *Nightfall* squared away once more for the Haven Bar buoy.

'I had this happen to me once,' said D, showing me the broken fitting. 'And mine was also a bronze screw. Look here, you can see the metal is crystallised where it's fractured. That's the trouble with these yellow metal fittings, you never know just how sound the metal is beneath the polished surface,' and he gave me a wry smile. 'I prefer honest to goodness galvanised screws, don't you?'

'I've learnt my lesson,' I admitted as I took my ship in between the shingle banks at the bar, heading her for the two white metes in line on the beach. 'This sloop rig with no runners may be all right for the Broads, but it won't do at sea. And I'll replace those four rigging screws with iron ones.'

Suddenly the roaring of the waves on the shingle banks ceased to fill our ears, and there came a sudden hush, as if a radio had been switched off. We were in the river itself now, the tumult of the bar was astern and blanketed by the high beach of shingle on our starboard beam, and here we ran almost along its edge, so steep to is it, in dead silence except for the soft rustling of the dinghy astern.

That night we lay in Butley River in about a fathom, close to the old brick dock, the only boat in sight.

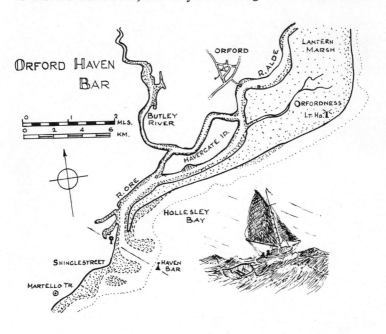

'Tomorrow morning we'll go up to Aldeburgh,' I told my shipmate, 'and have a word with the yard there. We jolly nearly lost our mast today, and would have done if you hadn't put her round so smartly, D. It's been a lesson to me,' I added to avoid his blushes, 'and I'm going to change her to cutter rig.'

'Fit a new forestay from the stem to the hounds,' he queried, 'and a pair of running backstays? She'll be a much better boat for it.'

And next day, while the branch line train jogged along to Saxmundham where we were to pick up the express to London, D and I made sketches of the changes I should make to *Nightfall*'s rig. And before that season was much older, and I had brought her back to Maldon before a happy easterly breeze, she emerged from Dan Webb's yard with as handy a gaff cutter rig and a new jib and forestaysail as anyone could wish for. And she and I were to share together many wonderful fair wind passages around the East Coast, and not a few minor adventures, during the five years that I owned her.

6

By the Havengore route

For the best part of a week, when I took my usual lunch hour stroll with sandwiches through the Temple Gardens down to the Embankment, strong sou'westerly winds had been whipping up white horses over the muddy water below Westminster Bridge, and the trees in the Gardens had been swaying and roaring in the blasts. It was surely to be hoped that this series of deep depressions which the BBC had been forecasting with their usual gusto would blow themselves out before the weekend, for Bill had arranged to meet me on the Friday evening at Liverpool Street station so as to join *Nightfall* at Pin Mill for ten days' break away from our respective offices.

My trusty old shipmate Duncan was to have joined us also at Pin Mill, but through some last minute changes being made at his bank (he was in fact about to become manager) he found to our mutual sorrow that he couldn't get away this time. Nonetheless, I was happy to have an old colleague like Bill with me, for he shared my love of the more remote haunts of our East Coast, and was always amiable and sympathetic towards my own preference for the less strenuous ways of cruising.

We both had to admit, however, that with ten full days before having to return to our desk jobs many of our more enthusiastic sailing friends would have seized this opportunity to plan an ambitious cruise across to the other side of the North Sea, taking in Dunkirk or Ostende and Flushing, and perhaps along the Middelburg Canal at least as far as charming little Veere, before heading back for home. But

happily for his skipper's peace of mind Bill harboured no
desire to pack as much passage-making as possible into a
limited time, and as *Nightfall* was still without any mechanical
propulsion other than her springy sweep, he said he was just
as content as I was to potter along the coast and explore its
creeks and little islands.

'Besides,' he added as we stowed our gear on the Friday
evening and made *Nightfall*'s pleasant panelled cabin look
warm and homely again, 'I'd love to make that passage
through Havengore that you've spoken of, if we're bound for
the Thames. I've never even seen the place. Could we do that,
do you think?'

It certainly agreed with the general plan I had had in
mind, for with the weather pattern still evidently unsettled an
inside passage cruise like that seemed to hold out more enjoyable possibilities than the chance of being cooped up weatherbound in some odorous harbour on the Belgian or Dutch
coast. Pleasant harbours given over solely to yachts with all
the amenities were still years away.

'D'you notice the wind's gone a bit more westerly,' my
good shipmate remarked as we got our little vessel underway
the following morning. 'The glass has risen a bit during the
night, and I do beleive it's taking off.'

As *Nightfall* with three rolls in her mainsail rounded
Collimer Point and began to fetch down towards Harwich on
a close reach, the result of more than a week of continuous
gales was laid out in force before us — a wonderful sight.
Anchored under the lee of Shotley Spit and stretching almost
half way up Sea Reach lay a fleet of barges, in singles and in
pairs alongside each other, bobs at their mastheads streaming
in the wind. We had to count them again and again as we leant
on our way past their sterns.

'I make it thirty-four, no thirty-five,' said Bill, 'I've never
seen so many barges together before. I wonder why they're
not getting underway on this tide with the wind easing like
this, for they must all be bound up for the London River,
don't you think?'

I began to wonder also at the apparent inactivity, for the
wind had definitely drawn more westerly, and the murky sky
to windward certainly looked like clearing. If that was going to

be the case, and our optimism made us confident that this was so, then this last depression would be on its way over, and in an hour or two the wind should have veered into the nor'west, with a clearing sky and bright clouds racing across it.

That would give us just the slant we wanted to make the Spitway and thence fetch up the Whitaker Channel into the Crouch. It would also be just what most of those barge skippers must have been waiting for for this past week or more. Then why, the nagging little doubt persisted as we stretched past the ancient outline of Harwich town and headed for the Naze, why was not a single one of those spritties following us out of the harbour? Like a tiresome phone bell ringing somewhere the old rhyme jingled at the back of my mind: 'First rise after low foretells a stronger blow', and I began to wonder if I was being over-reckless or just plain stupid to ignore these signs.

In less than an hour, when *Nightfall* was barely two miles beyond Walton and we could just make out the end of Clacton pier to windward, the heavens gave us the answer. To the westward the sky had become a deep slate grey, and with a cold blast that whipped the white crests off the Wallet seas the wind flew into its old quarter, tearing at us straight out of the sou'west, and dead in our teeth. *Nightfall* lay over as if astonished at the weight in this rising wind, and the leech of the mainsail started to quiver with a sound like distant gunfire.

'OK, Bill, roll up the jib, will you, while I get a few more turns in the mains'l.' I already had the helm down and a slipline on it.

'Turning back are we?' My shipmate hove in on the jib furling line and got the flogging sail to sleep. 'Nothing else for it, is there?'

Good old Bill, I thought, no arguing, no recriminations, just a quiet acceptance of the situation. It was certainly going to be no day for a small cutter to be threshing to windward out here, and under easier canvas with five rolls in the mains'l and the boom stays'l set, *Nightfall* bore away and began to run like a startled hind back towards Harwich. It was somewhere about here a few years previously, I recalled that another shipmate and I had had to wrestle with my old smack *Afrina* when a squall just like this one pulled the starboard bowsprit shroud plate right out of the poor old smack's side, and we almost lost the long bowsprit*. We had run back on that occasion, too, with leaky boltholes in our bow.

'By Jove, Maurice,' Bill grinned as he wiped his spectacles. 'It really is blowing. Look at the spray blowing away to loo'ard from the bow, just like smoke.'

Nightfall, usually the most docile of boats, was behaving as one possessed, and at times it was all I could do at the tiller, even with the line wrapped around it, to keep her from broaching-to. We could well have done with yet a couple more rolls in the mains'l, but with Harwich only a few miles away and the wind on our port quarter with no fear of a sudden gybe, we just let her race back the way we had come. But I was more than thankful for the change to cutter rig and the running backstays I had had fitted since that episode outside Orford Haven bar.

The barges, every one of them, were still there when we ran past Shotley Spit and rushed past their disdainful sterns with our tails, so to speak, between our legs. And we were happy to round up close to the weather shore above the last of the spritties and let go the anchor.

'I ought to know by now,' I admitted ruefully, 'that if you only watch what the bargemen are doing, you won't go far wrong. Those old chaps know more about weather signs than even the BBC boys.'

'But it was a damn fine sail,' Bill chuckled, 'while it lasted!'

And so it came to pass that, after a blustery night when our anchor cable stretched out ahead in the darkness like an iron bar and the squalls rose at times to a wild shriek in our rigging, we were awakened in the early morning by familiar sounds — the rhythmic clink-clink-clink of windlass pawls, and the spasmodic clack-clack-clack of patent sheaves as tops'ls were being hoisted.

'Oh boy, it's a wonderful sight,' exclaimed Bill with his head out of the hatch. 'The whole lot are getting underway.'

It was indeed a sight that I have long since cherished in my sailing memories. The expected break in the weather had come at last, and the morning was bright with a pale sun rising

Magic of the Swatchways

over the Trimley marshes and the blue sky speckled with little clouds hurrying before a smart nor'westerly wind. This was clearly the change the barge skippers had been waiting for, and as we watched the massed crowd of masts and sprits which we had passed and re-passed the day before was now rapidly separating. As brails were let go with a run, mainsails were unfolding like stage curtains at a theatre, tops'ls were rising jerkily to mastheads, and foresail sheets were crashing across the iron horse as each barge payed off on the starboard tack, while anchors dripping black river mud, rose to stemheads.

In no time at all, it seemed, all the barges were turning their sterns towards us as they leant over to the wind and began to stretch out of the harbour, sailing in line ahead like a well drilled fleet. From the foremost to the laggards last in the line there must have been a full mile of barges, spaced out at intervals, and all of them hurrying at long last out towards the Naze. With the flood tide soon to start running southward with them they would be able to fetch up Swin and carry their tide all the way with them into Medway or Thames as far as they were bound.

Suddenly the anchorage seemed as empty as a desert with *Nightfall* the only little vessel left. This shift of wind would suit our purpose as well as the barges', and after a hurried breakfast we had the anchor up, and under full mains'l, stays'l and jib we were soon chasing the last of the spritties as she cleared the harbour entrance. It seemed a long chase out towards the Naze, and I thought of the youthful Captain Nelson working his sixth-rate under a local pilot's directions on a taut bowline out from Harwich through this shallow channel which today carries on the chart the name of his command, *Medusa*, to avoid the longer plug round the Cork sands on his way at orders from Admiralty to report to Chatham forthwith.

Gradually we overhauled the slower of the barges ahead and lay on a reach with three of them together through the narrow Spitway between the Gunfleet and the Buxey sands. Then we came more on the wind to fetch up the Whitaker channel past the tall black beacon with a topmark like a half-opened umbrella, while the barges went their way up Swin. As

69

far as the eye could see the line of brown sails seemed to fill the horizon through our lee rigging, the leaders so far below the horizon that only their tops'ls could be made out above the glinting wave tops.

'Havengore, is it to be Maurice?' Bill quizzed me through his hornrims and looked relieved when I nodded.

As the day wore on and the breeze began to soften *Nightfall* found her way into the Roach and, rustling happily in the smooth water between the sedge-covered banks, she came into Yokefleet Creek between Potton and Foulness islands and on through the winding channel of Narrow Cuts until the iron drawbridge across the fairway barred further progress. Here she rounded up, folded her brown wings and came to rest with her anchor down, while her skipper and mate went ashore in the dinghy to ask the bridgekeeper about depths of water and the chance of going through on the morning's tide.

'Should have plenty of water,' Jim the bridgeman told us. 'There was four foot today's tide, should be a few inches more tomorrow, seein' they's still on the make. Three foot and a bit, you say you draw, why you ought be able to go out around ten o'clock.'

As we settled back on board, sitting in the cockpit as the tide fell and *Nightfall* nestled comfortably and almost upright on the soft muddy bottom, nothing could have been more peaceful than this little creek. The dying breeze wafted scents of the land towards us, of marram grass and flowers and earth smells from a nearby farm, while the trilling of a lark, hardly visible against the blue sky, and the melancholy lowing of cows in the meadows, were soothing sounds that belonged only to nature.

For me, and I think equally for my companion, this settling down to wait for the tide to run its course out into the North Sea, and then on the flood to come welling up into the creek again, was no hardship, for us no waste of time, but one of the many quiet enjoyments of this ditch-crawling way of cruising. If I harboured any qualms that we were not dyed-in-the-wool cruising men, having no thirst to voyage across the seas to far distant ports, I could call to mind others who shared a love of these peaceful creeks and quiet, lonely anchorages.

One whom I knew well was Francis B Cooke, whose several books on small boat cruising have delighted and instructed newcomers to the sport for many years. With a job in the City like my own in not allowing any long breaks away from the desk, he spent almost all his sailing days between his base for many years at Fambridge and the Medway in the south and Aldeburgh to the north; and in this coastal pottering, as he more than once told me, he was completely happy. One week-end in a friend's boat on the Solent, and one trip to Ostende and Flushing in another's yacht gave him, he said, all the experience he wished for of distant cruising; the rest of the time he was happy to explore the rivers and creeks of the Essex and Suffolk coasts, and he retained his love of these waters until the day he passed away, full of years and pleasant memories, at the age of one hundred and two.

'Instead of sitting here,' I remarked a little mischievously, 'we could have followed all those barges and carried our flood with them up Swin and well up the Thames or the Medway. Wouldn't you have felt nobler doing that, or even heading for the Noord Hinder lightvessel and the Dutch coast with yesterday's swell still bucking at us?'

'What, and miss this peaceful anchorage?' Bill's chuckle was infectious. 'I'd far rather sit waiting like this for the kettle to boil and watch that old heron standing at the edge of the creek over there. Isn't he fine?'

The motionless statue, like that of a little old man in a grey frock coat, suddenly darted at the water, and with a flurry of outstretched wings sailed upward and away, a fish clutched in his beak and his long legs stretched out behind him. We watched his flight as he soared over the bank with stately wing beats and settled somewhere out of sight, and a great contentment seemed to spread over the evening shadows.

The early morning beamed upon us like a freshly washed face, for the sun was bright, the sky an intense blue, and a nice whole sail breeze was shepherding clouds in little groups from out of the north west. For some time the flood tide had been flowing in from the Crouch and Roach, stirring our little ship from her night's berth; but as the watershed in the creek beyond the road bridge became covered, the tidal stream came to a standstill and then started to flow in from the sea.

Nightfall noticed this and turned herself slowly to face it, pointing her bowsprit towards the Thames where the waters sparkled in the sunshine, and almost on the horizon big ships were passing each other on their lawful voyages, some going up to the docks of London, others outward bound for all places on the earth.

With mainsail tiers loosened and the anchor almost broken out, we waited while two or three cars and a military truck rumbled across the bridge span, for this road was the only link between the mainland at Shoebury and the closely guarded War Department area on Foulness Island. Then the span began to rise slowly on its hinges, and to a wave from the bridgekeeper *Nightfall* under her mains'l and jib nosed her way through the widening gap and between the steep banks of the creek beyond, until she began to feel, imperceptibly at

'Nightfall' spreads her wings at Havengore Bridge

first, the slight heaving of the sea.

Bill sat by the weather shrouds deftly sounding with the striped pole.

'Four feet. Four. Four again. Must be as flat as a pancake.'

Off the mouth of the channel a ricketty-looking post with a double cross topmark like a printer's asterisk slid past a few yards away. According to old charts, which can be seen at the British Museum, there has been some sort of seamark on this spot for centuries, and marked as the Orwell Beacon. How it got its name is only conjecture, but at least as late as the eighteenth century this channel leading past the gore or spit of Foulness was wider and deeper than it is today, and shallow-draught vessels could work their way through by this route into the Crouch and thence to Harwich and the Orwell, and so save the often rough and tedious plug round Foulness and Whitaker sands. The haven at the gore would doubtless be crowded with small shipping come a black no'theaster that can blight these waters, even in summer!

'Isn't there a cart track or something called the Broom-way' asked Bill, 'somewhere hereabouts?'

'We've probably just about sailed over it,' I answered. 'It's been shown on old charts for centuries, and I believe it's still used sometimes by the farmers on the island. The chart shows it as a roadway leading from off the beach at Shoobrie — as it used to be — over the sand for about three miles and up to the sea wall on to Foulness. In old days,' I added, warming to my subject, 'it was marked by rows of short besom-topped stakes or brooms — like the channels around the Frisian islands you remember in Childers' *Riddle of the Sands* — and they used to call them mapples. With those shallow pools that are left by the tide called linns, it's been argued that is how these Maplin sands got their name.'

Feeling like a satisfied schoolmaster who has just delivered a lesson to a receptive class, I was brought down to earth with a bump. And another bump, which had all the rigging rattling. And bump again. Bill slid the pole overboard in a trice.

'Less water here, skipper. Barely three and a half feet.'

A fourth time *Nightfall*'s keel juddered on the sand as her bow rose and fell languidly over a slight swell left over from some passing steamer's wash, which I had been too busy pontificating to notice. It was happily only a short series of bumps, a classic example of the phrase 'touch and go', for *Nightfall* didn't quite stop, but began to forge ahead again when the last of the swells had rolled past.

'My goodness,' said my companion thoughtfully, 'it makes you realize how hard these sands are, and how quickly a yacht could break up if she got on them in a gale o'wind. Makes you shiver to think of it.'

We had talked of trying to get as far on this flood tide as we could so as to bring up in Hadleigh Ray for the night. Ever since I had owned my much-loved little bawley cutter *Storm*, I had intended to visit Bundock's yard at Leigh-on-Sea where she had been built for some owner back in 1910, but so far had never made it. Now this cruise seemed to offer the ideal opportunity and Bill, I was glad to note, was more than happy to have a look at the ancient fishing town of Leigh. But as I pointed out, we were paying the penalty of creeping through the Havengore route, instead of carrying the whole of the flood up Swin and straight up to Leigh. For you cannot get out of Havengore until nearly high water, and here we were with but an hour's fair tide to run.

'We'll have to lay as close as we can to Shoeburyness,' I said, 'and cheat the tide as much as possible along the shore. If we can make the end of Southend Pier — and that's a mile and a quarter out from the shore — and this wind holds, then we ought to be able to work up over the ebb into the entrance to the Ray.'

'We'll have a bash, skipper.' My companion was of the stuff of which good cruising men are made. 'And if we find we can't do it, what then?'

'We'll have to bear away a little across the ebb for the mouth of the Medway.'

And in the event we didn't make the Ray that day, for little by little our brave nor'westerly breeze became shy under the influence of the sun, and soon the strong Thames ebb was making further progress to windward less and less praiseworthy. With no engine to help it was profitless to try beating up towards the long pier, and we both agreed to give it best and leave till tomorrow's tide to get over to *Storm*'s birthplace.

Slanting across the estuary with the ebb pressing down on our weather bow, *Nightfall* just managed to make the East Nore Sand buoy, while the red hull of the Nore itself — the very first moored lightship in the world, I believe, and placed there since 1732 — appeared to be closing up on us yard by yard. But *Nightfall* hugged the edge of Grain Spit as the Martello tower slid past, while the ebb pouring out of the Medway pulled at her hull like a reluctant child being dragged to the dentist.

For a time we thought of carrying on to find an anchorage close in shore near Victoria Pier, where the Royal Corinthian YC had its first clubhouse before it moved across the Estuary to Burnham-on-Crouch, but the ebb was too strong, and in the end we bore away and ran into the entrance to the West Swale. Here below the town causeway our anchor was let go and *Nightfall* seemed to sigh as we folded her wings and called it a day.

With the faltering breeze still in the north-west it would be quiet enough here, while at least the glue factory which makes the Queenborough anchorage such a memorable place in easterly winds, was to leeward. We needed paraffin and more stores, and this gave us an excuse to row ashore and explore the depressing streets of the little town, but neither of us being pub-loving people we were soon back on board discussing our plans for the morrow.

Barges away with a fair slant

7

Slowly into the Swale

The way into Leigh Creek

'There's the Low Way buoy, fine on the bow' said Bill, 'and according to Irving we leave that to port and go in NW by N for Leigh church. And look,' he added, holding up the blue-covered book, 'here's a lovely little sketch on page six of Leigh church standing on the hill above the trees. And there it is, a square tower just as the book shows it.'

With a light westerly filling her sails *Nightfall* had started early that morning and had worked out of the West Swale and down past Grain Spit as the young flood was beginning to run. Coming hard on the wind she had managed to lay nicely through the Jenkin Swatch on the port tack, and then freed her sheets to stretch across Sea Reach and its busy shipping, with the tide now helping her under her lee bow. And in my experience that is the best place for a friendly tide to be.

The extensive flats of the Southend and Leigh foreshore ahead of us were already covered, but the small black buoys showed us where the Ray Gut lay so as to lead us into the entrance to Leigh Creek. Away to port three or four of the big local bawleys with cut down masts, together with a few local yachts farther up at their moorings, indicated the lay of Hadleigh Ray, which runs up as an ever narrowing creek inside the Small Gains saltings of Canvey Island.

As Bill had remarked, Commander John Irving's book was proving an essential guide to exploring these Estuary waters when used in conjunction with those fine coloured charts issued specially for yachtsmen by Imrays of the Minories. Some of Irving's chapters had been appearing as a series of sailing directions in the *Yachting Monthly,* and shortly after I had become its editor it was arranged for them to be published in a handy volume, *Rivers and Creeks of the Thames Estuary,* which appeared in 1927. With the clearly inscribed charts backed by delightful recognition sketches of approaches and sea marks drawn by Beryl, John's artist wife, *Rivers and Creeks* was a worthy successor to the long-out-of-print book by Messum, and we were glad to have it on board with us. Almost thirty years, in fact, were to elapse before Irving's book was to go out of print in its turn and to be superseded by another *Yachting Monthly* publication, Jack H Coote's *East Coast Rivers,* which as I write has gone into its ninth edition, and must be used by thousands of East Coast yachtsmen.

The creek ahead of us turned and twisted like a petrified eel, but following Irving's notes we edged our way past one withy shaking in the tide after another, until a small hand-crane on a stone jetty with a large clinker-built beach boat alongside, caught our eye. This, we agreed, must be Bell Wharf and the town landing place. While I quickly stowed the mainsail, Bill rounded *Nightfall* up against the tide and laid her alongside the quay with neither a bump nor a scratch.

A longshoreman in seaboots, blue jersey and a battered peaked cap over a surprisingly honest-looking face agreed that he would keep a heye on the bo't fer a pint-like, and we left her in his charge for a tour of exploration. Across the path by the old London, Tilbury & Southend Railway station we came across Bundock Bros' yard looking like many another old boatyard, with stacks of timber seasoning in the open, weathered moulds like mock-up bulkheads from various craft built here stacked against a wall, a big tarred weatherboarded shed with a leaky corrugated iron roof, and through a doorway inside the ecclesiastical gloom of a church where there was a prevading smell of freshly sawn pine, wood shavings, paint and pitch.

From beyond the further doorway leading to the shore came the dull thud of a caulking mallet. 'It would probably be in this shed,' I remarked 'that my old *Storm* was built, and that was in the same year as *Nightfall*, 1910. She was just a small edition of the fine old bawleys that used to be built here all those years ago. But there doesn't seem to be much building now, does there?'

On the foreshore beyond the shed which led steeply down to the creek we came across a young fellow who was hammering cotton caulking into the open seams of an ancient cutter yacht which was propped up on legs. He told us he had worked at the yard only a few months, he didn't know where the guv'nor was, out buying some timber he thought, nor whether they had any orders for fishing boats; no, boats wasn't really his interest-like, he was keen on motorbikes himself, never had cared for boats much, but it was a job-like, wasn't it?

We retraced our steps along the cinderpath that led between the railway fencing and the creek, while I thought of the old days when Leigh was the home of dozens of fine bawleys and many more small shrimpers and cocklers. The Leigh bawleys were a type of their own, powerful vessels with straight stems and wide transom sterns, ranging in size between 10m by 3.5m to about 12m by 4.5m beam with a draught of 1.7m or so. They were rigged with a loose-sheeted mainsail, that is, it had a very long gaff giving the sail an almost vertical leech with no boom, and the parts of the mainsheet were led to a great double block with its own belaying pin running over an iron horse across the transom.

On a separate topmast, which was usually bowsed slightly forward like a barge's, a big topsail, a real working sail, was set, while the forestays'l usually worked again like a barge's over an iron horse across the foredeck. When trawling for shrimps or white fish in the Estuary the bawleys set a small jib part of the way along the great bowsprit in the manner of the Colchester and Mersea oyster smacks. But when Leigh Town regatta came round, the bawleys would break out the most surprising sails like long-footed tow fores'ls and huge white jib tops'ls, and a dozen or more of them would make a memorable sight as they fought each other across the starting line. When they were out shrimping the men boiled their catch ready for the London market, and it was a familiar enough sight for a group of these fine vessels to be trawling below Southend pier with the smoke from their chimneys blowing away to leeward and carrying the smell of the boiling shrimps. It has been said that this is how these boiler boats came to be called bawleys.

The smaller Leigh cocklers, on the other hand, worked from the narrow creek leading up past Bell Wharf to the steep beach on which a picturesque row of wooden sheds in various stages of disrepair sported grotesque chimneys from their boiler plants. It was the work of these boats, which ranged from about 26ft (7.9m) to 32ft (9.8m) to sail on the ebb down to the Maplins or the Foulness sands and settle on the ground as the tide left them. The men scoured the sand around with wide rakes and shovelled the sand and cockles mixture into the open hold until the boat was full. As soon as the flood returned and the boats refloated they set all the sail they could carry — and their rig was an exact copy of the bawley's — and raced each other back to the creek. To be first afloat and first back alongside the sheds was of paramount importance, for it meant catching the best of the orders. For this reason cocklers were built with fine sailing hulls and almost flat bottoms, drawing less than a metre, and a great iron centreplate with its case divided the hold space completely down the middle.

In due time, of course, motor driven cocklers with stump masts swept away the lofty rigs of the older boats, and the bawleys themselves eventually disappeared from the scene, to be replaced by a new race of young fishermen with their powerful diesel trawlers. In a minor way I was glad to have been instrumental in recording for posterity what many of these local fishing boats had been like before the internal combustion engine had usurped all the sailing craft. Through the efforts of the late W Maxwell Blake, a designer of a number of healthy cruising yachts and a superb draughtsman, lines were taken off dozens of old fishing craft and small coasters around the British coasts, and these appeared with suitable notes as a series in the *Yachting Monthly* from about 1930 until the outbreak of the Hitler war. Later, it was gratifying to learn that after his death prints of Maxwell Blake's fishing boat plans were made available to the public from the Maritime Section of the Science Museum, South Kensington.

At one of the sheds along the cinder path, and attracted by a rhythmic *shush-shush* noise, Bill and I looked in to watch how the cockles were separated from their shells by being rocked to and fro through a steam jet in a large square sieve which was hung on rods from the roof. Whether or not the gritty little cockle or the larger rubbery whelk well soused in vinegar is pronounced a delicacy depends upon on one's individual taste, or perhaps one's geographical upbringing, but that this is a very ancient local industry is indicated by old records which show that the fishermen held rights in Leigh Creek since the time of Henry VIII. But in those days the creek was probably much wider and deeper than the muddy gully it is today.

Watching the big, thigh-booted jersied fishermen emptying their baskets of cockle shells on to the enormous heaps outside the sheds reminded me of A E Copping's engaging story of Leigh in the days before the First World War. In *Gotty and the Guv'nor* he described how, as a City gent with a love for sailing and fishing, he bought one of the bawleys and employed as his skipper Gotty, a well known local character, and made of it a highly entertaining story full of Essex dialect and bawley lore.

Memory plays many useless tricks on the advanced in age, but the foreshore at Leigh-on-Sea always remind me of another book which I found in a library when I had just started to learn sailing. It was a modest volume of short cruises in these waters in a little 4-ton cutter with the title *Swale, Swin and Swatchway*, published about 1894, but I cannot recall the author's name nor have I ever seen another copy. However, thinking of sailing exploits in the Thames Estuary one cannot overlook Francis B Cooke's *In Tidal Waters*, published in 1919 with superb illustrations by C Fleming Williams.

And how well those old professional illustrators served readers and editors of magazines and books in those days.

There has been nothing, in my view, to equal the splendid technical illustrations drawn of current events by these artists for such periodicals as the *Illustrated London News, The Graphic, The Sphere* and many other high class magazines. Compared with some of these drawings of events no camera shot of today can capture the atmosphere or the detail. In my own early days first on a fortnightly paper, then with the monthly magazine, I was in the enviable position of being able to reproduce the work of a number of fine illustrators whose pictures could be relied upon to capture the very essence of the sea and little ships and the kind of men who sailed them. I recall with gratitude such names as W L Wyllie, Arthur Briscoe, Chas Pears, H Alker Tripp, W Edward Wigfull (who lived up the hill at Leigh), Robert E Groves, George F Holmes, Archie White, S I Veale, Winston Megoran, Leslie A Wilcox, and Fid Harnack, who was later to transform one or two of my own books with his lively illustrations.

When I think how the true-to-life work of such artists brought a splendid individuality and freshness to the pages of any periodical, I feel saddened when looking at popular magazines of today with their vast spreads of photographic close-ups, their pages of nothing but camera pictures, with only just enough reading matter that will tie the photographs together and not tax the reader's brain. But, according to one contemporary school of thought, it may be that before long there will be no need for any man to have to *read*: as a child he will learn, communicate, record entirely electronically. And he will have lost one of life's great pleasures.

'The tide, oh skipper,' Bill's voice reminded me, 'it waiteth not upon the sloth of any man.'

He was right to break in upon my sad thoughts, for it would soon be high water, and with such a tricky channel to negotiate down to the deeps of the Ray Gut we didn't want to tarry until the ebb had set in and run the risk of spending the next twelve hours at an angle on the mud flats. After a hurried sandwich and a beer in the Peter Boat on the waterside — at that time this ancient pub had not yet been 'modernised' — we bought half a pound of freshly smoked cod's roe for two shillings (10p) at one of the fishermen's huts, paid off our watchman on the wharf, and pushed off on the last of the tide.

As it happened we need not have bothered so much about retracing the winding course of the creek, for in the time Bill and I had been exploring Leigh town the tide had risen sufficiently for *Nightfall* with her shallow draught to have sailed almost anywhere over the mud flats. From abreast Southend's long pier the light westerly breeze carried her slanting across the lee running ebb while she headed over the Cant and the Four Fathom Channel towards the sandy bluff of Warden Point on Sheppey Isle.

We were not bound far today, for our plans were again modest in the extreme, and we had both decided to try to make into the East Swale so as to be able to spend the night at an anchorage off Harty Ferry which neither of us had visited for some years. The reason, truth to tell, was partly sentimental as Bill reminded me.

'I shall never forget,' he said, 'the last time you and I lay at Harty Ferry in your old *Storm,* and we had that marvellous sail across the Estuary that night. D'you remember, skipper, we'd been aground on the tail of the Horse all afternoon, while it blew a gale from the west'ard, and then at sunset — and what a beautiful sunset that was — the wind eased and the sky cleared. And then we set off at high water for the Wallet Spitway and the Blackwater. D'you remember,' he added, blinking at me as he wiped his glasses, 'what a lovely starry night it was, with all that phosphorescence on the water? It was like the Milky Way running past the rudder.'

Bill's poetical description was infectious.

'Ah, the sea and the stars, and the silence of the night,' I found myself saying. 'What wonders are there for those who go down to the sea in little ships. Yes, you don't often have nights like that in these northern climes. Maybe I should write about that night sometime.' And in due time I did, in *The Magic of the Swatchways.*

Bill was poring over the Imray coloured chart.

'Look, how did some of these sands and channels in the Thames Estuary get their names? Look there, there's the Spile and the Cant, which we've just sailed across, and the Spaniard, the Gilman, Pan Sand, the Tongue, Pudding Pan, Girdler, Studhill, the Last, the Mouse, the Knob — North and East of that — and the Barrow.' He traced a finger along one of the channels. 'Here's the Kentish Knock. Why Knock? The Shivering Sand I could guess as made up of quicksands, but I'd like to know how on earth, and why, the Woolpack shoal just nor'west of the Hook Sand got its name. And take the Columbine Spit the other side of Ham Gat that we're now heading for: who on earth was Columbine?'

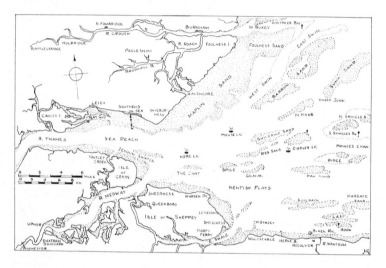

Thames Estuary, the Crouch to the Swale

Admitting a state of ignorance which has always depressed me, I said honestly I just didn't know, but hazarded the guess that the Columbine might have got its name from the wreck of some mediaeval ship of that name, like possibly the Spaniard. Shoals with names like the Long Sand, the Sunk, the Red Sand, Tongue and Ridge could, I thought, be guessed from their general shape and position, while sands called the Knob and the Knowl would surely be isolated rounded banks like a head or knob. And a few years later I found a fascinating little book, *A Short History of the Thames Estuary* by H Muir Evans (Imrays), which discussed the origins of these very names with reproductions of parts of old charts dating from Wagenhaer 1584 to Admiralty surveys of the nineteenth century.

'The ebb's fairly running out of here, isn't it,' Bill

remarked as we hauled our sheets a little and crept slowly past the most easterly point of Sheppey with the apt name of Shell Ness. Away to port, through the lee rigging, the Whitstable Flats were uncovering, and in the hazy distance we could just make out the thin line that marked Whitstable Street. A natural tidemade phenomenon, it forms a kind of finger of sand and gravel that juts out from the beach in a northerly direction for about a mile. It is a hard well used by the local fishermen, and although submerged at high water it nevertheless gives a welcome shelter to the smacks which lie on the flats hereabouts. We could see three or four of them now, with their masts at rakish angles as the tide left them, and thought of the days when there were thirty or forty of these fine oyster dredgers regularly working over these flats, with the police boat, usually a smart cutter, in attendance to prevent poaching. The three local shipyards were busy then building and repairing these smacks as well as the occasional Thames barge and coasting schooner.

Through the binoculars Bill was studying the little jetty which marked the entrance to the harbour some two miles away across the quickly drying flats.

'I've never been inside the harbour,' he said. 'It dries right out, and the tide's never been right. I wonder if any ships use the place now, or d'you reckon it's practically died as a port, like Felixstowe Dock?'

I said I had once or twice seen barges in there, and an odd coaster or two, but there didn't seem to be much trade these days. He swigged in the jibsheet while I overhauled a little on the main, for we were steadily coming more on the wind as we pointed up Swale.

'How old is the harbour,' asked Bill, for he liked to pursue a subject to its conclusion. 'And why was it built, anyway?'

Amongst my collection of books on early railways at home I recalled reading how the citizens of Canterbury had been impressed with the success of the first public steam railway, the Stockton and Darlington, and had decided to enlarge the tiny harbour on the coast at Whitstable and to build a railway themselves from this dock the eight miles to Canterbury, so as to avoid the scandalous charges made by the road hauliers for everything brought into their town, and especially sea coal.

The Canterbury and Whitstable Railway was the result, and it was opened, the third of its kind, a few months after the Liverpool and Manchester in 1830.

This little line had to climb over high ground between the harbour and the city, and at first trains of loaded wagons and a passenger coach or two were hauled up the steep inclines by stationary engines and ropes, but on the more level section at the harbour end haulage was by a small steam locomotive, the *Invicta*. Looking like a road tar boiler with its four wheels and very tall chimney, this primitive six-ton machine followed closely on the building of Stephenson's famous *Rocket* in 1829, and it is still in existence, mounted on a plinth in Canterbury.

Before many years this short branch was absorbed by the South Eastern Railway and more powerful locomotives, specially built, replaced the rope haulage throughout. Meanwhile Whitstable Harbour flourished with the trade brought to it by barges and coasters to be transported to Canterbury and other parts of Kent, and for many years its quays were always crowded. But gradually the business fell away as the growing network of railways took over from the coastwise traffic, and the little port fell into Victorian decline.

We continued to work our way over the ebb until we had almost reached the first of the small yachts on moorings abreast of the Harty Ferry, and here the hook was let go and the sails stowed.

'Very nearly where we brought up last time in *Storm*,' Bill remarked looking round the anchorage. 'But this time,' he added with a sly grin, 'let's try to keep off the Horse, eh skipper?'

A row round in the dinghy to look at some of the unfamiliar yachts, and then a landing at the Hard and a pleasant walk between hedgerows and along the lane towards Leysdown helped us to stretch our legs and work up an appetite for one of Bill's delicious suppers.

Sitting contentedly in the cockpit while Bill puffed at his pipe, we watched the sun go down behind the distant haze of the Medway cement works with every sign of a fine day on the morrow. Then we turned in, tired but contented, with the prospect of taking the morning's ebb along the coast to the

North Foreland, and if we timed it properly we should be able to catch the first of the south-running flood round the headland.

'Then where?' Bill asked sleepily.

'Pegwell Bay, perhaps,' I suggested. 'We've never been up the Stour to Sandwich, have we? And we'd better get to some place where we can get some more paraffin.'

But Bill, like the evening outside, seemed already asleep.

8

Calm off the Roman coast

'You wouldn't think,' said Bill, 'that all last week it was blowing gales of wind. One after another. And now, look at this,' and he swept his arm round at the glassy sea.

There was a slight haze over the land, and the houses and hotels on top of the cliffs at Herne Bay looked faint and ghostly in the midday sun. Since we had got underway that morning our passage out of the Swale and past the shore off Whitstable had been a slow one with only a light baffling air from out of the North. It was almost entirely the tide which was helping us to make good our course along the Kentish shore towards the eastward. And even these fickle breaths had finally died away, and now *Nightfall* was floating in a calm so complete that we ventured to leave her with her sails hanging limp while we pushed off in the dinghy with the camera to try to get a shot or two of her.

When the ripples from the little boat had died away our home of the week sat motionless before us, her inverted image reflected in perfection, so that our pictures of her could be described as double-takes. It was a pity that colour photographs had not yet come into common use, for recalling Coleridge's oft quoted lines:

> *We stuck, nor breath nor motion,*
> *As idle as a painted ship*
> *Upon a painted ocean,*

my little ship that day appeared to me a perfect picture.

We rowed quietly round her discussing her workmanlike

lines and the features we liked, and admitting those that in our eyes were not so good. It is not often that an owner gets a chance thus to study his boat as others see her, and it must be a bemused fellow who cannot see faults that could be corrected. On the whole *Nightfall* seemed to me all I could want — well, nearly all — for my way of weekend and odd days cruising around the Thames Estuary, with her shallow draught and her ability to keep herself sailing on course with the tiller lashed while I busied myself with those innumerable jobs that every yacht demands. A good all-round cruising boat, she seemed to me, although with a critical eye I admitted I should have liked her with more sheer forward and a saucier lift to her cut-off counter, wider side decks with a higher foot-rail, and the mast perhaps eighteen inches farther aft. But then, I told myself unnecessarily, every boat has to be a compromise, and there was nothing I could do to improve *Nightfall* right now; and as is the way of things, after a few years more I parted with her so as to build a boat to one of my own designs. Some forty years later on I was happy to meet one of *Nightfall*'s subsequent owners who told me that the old yacht, well into her sixties by now, had made a highly enjoyable cruise by way of the Dutch waterways to the German Frisian islands and back, following much of the route of the *Dulcibella* described in Erskine Childers's immortal *Riddle of the Sands*. They had hit bad weather in the North Sea, he told me, and they were impressed by the way the old yacht shouldered her way over the waves, often sailing herself with no one at the helm, and with her light displacement managing to keep green water off her decks. She was a good boat and seemed to know how a cruising boat should look after her crew.

Bill was resting on his oars and gazing up at the scarlet streamer that hung limp from the masthead. So still was the air that the droplets of water from off the oarblades made little musical 'plops' on the water, while the sound of a dog barking excitedly on the beach came clearly across the water. But in the background there was another sound which could be felt rather than heard, a deep distant rumbling like continuous gunfire from very far away.

'D'you reckon those are ships in the Estuary?' Bill cocked an ear. 'How far off would they be, do you think?'

'About ten or twelve miles, I'd reckon. They're probably passing through either the Edinburgh Channel or the Princes. But you'd hardly expect to hear their engines quite so clearly at that distance, would you?'

'Not if they were steamers,' my shipmate replied. 'But I'll bet they're mostly motorships, and you know what a racket some of them make.'

He was right, for the day of the nearly silent steamship's triple expansion engines ('the good old up-and-downers') was already drawing to a close. Even a passenger ship's steam turbines could be heard for miles on occasion, while the big diesel freighter could sound at night like a freight train rumbling over a continuous girder bridge. Sharply, as we clambered back on board our ship, another sound punctuated the vibrant rumble like a mournful cry from across the water. Half a minute later there it was again.

'That'll be the Tongue lightvessel,' I said. 'One blast every thirty seconds. Maybe this mist is working in from the sea, and will grow thicker.'

'So long as it doesn't turn into a real thick fog, skipper, I don't mind, but if there's one thing gets me edgy at sea it is fog.'

In case it did come in thick we took bearings of the end of Herne Bay pier and of the high ground abreast of us at Hillborough, and were satified that the lines on the chart confirmed our present position as roughly in the middle of the Copperas Channel. Bill dropped the lead and let the line trail out astern before hauling it in again.

'Well' he said, 'this ebb's taking us a little north of east. How's that skipper?'

I agreed it was all right — we oughtn't to get set on to the Hook Sand just to the north of us provided we took an occasional sounding, just to check our drift. But we did, I thought, have to avoid allowing ourselves, especially on the ebb, to be set on to Black Rock, which was a patch of boulders about half a mile off the beach at Reculver, and which dried at low water.

'There's the twin towers, now,' said Bill, pointing through the starboard rigging, 'just coming out of the mist. We should be well clear of that shoal now, shouldn't we?'

The Saxon church with its pair of flat topped towers rising above the cliff of Reculver has been a distinctive seamark for mariners down the centuries. Roughly contemporary with St Cedd's chapel of St Peter-on-the-Wall by Bradwell, it had been built about the middle of the seventh century AD, and it too was constructed largely of bricks and stones and flints plentifully available from the ruins of the Roman settlement of Regulbium.

In the days of the Roman occupation this fortification marked the entrance to an important waterway, a river which then meandered through the Kentish countryside into the Stour by Sandwich, making the north eastern segment of land, Thanet, a true island. Sandwich was then an important seaport on the coast before it retreated inland, and there was a fairly constant trade with ports in the Lowlands and the Channel coast of Gaul.

The small vessels of the day were able to enter Pegwell Bay and work their way into the Thames by this handy inland route, and thereby cut off the long haul round the turbulent North Foreland with its strong and unpredictable tides. But gradually this river silted up, always in need of more water than it actually had, so that — as I have read — it earned its present name Wantsum; which just shows how historians will explain anything away if they can.

Becalmed off Reculver

For many centuries small craft had, in addition to this short cut, the benefit of a further inland route into the Thames, for by way of the East and West Swale they could cross the Medway and pass inside the Isle of Grain, coming out into London River by way of Yantlet Creek. Thence they would have to face anything that Sea Reach might have to throw at them, but at least they would be saved the outside route round the Columbine Spit, the northern bulge of Sheppey, and Grain Spit with its shoals at the Nore. A well-manned Roman galley could make this passage on the young flood tide from the Regulbium settlement up to the ford at Londinium (near the present Blackfriars), and be back again with the next ebb the same day.

With their astonishing organising ability and feats of engineering it is not surprising that the Romans, although not fundamentally a seafaring people, learnt the art of building strong seagoing ships early in their history, for the vast growth of their dominions throughout the Mediterranean and Europe called for well-organised sea routes. The Roman merchant vessel, the *corbita*, developed into a big, round bellied freighter of immense strength, carrying a large square-sail with a divided raffee topsail on a mast amidships, and a highly steeved foremast (or bowsprit) on which was set the *artemon*, a small squaresail used to aid the steering. Controlling one of these lumbering ships, which could carry anything up to six hundred tons of cargo, was no mean feat even with three men each on two steering oars — one to port, the other on the normal steerboard side. It was in such a ship, with 275 other people on board, that St Paul was being escorted under arrest to Rome for questioning when he was driven by a storm lasting many days on to the shores of the island of Melita, the present Malta.

That the shipmasters of the Roman Empire learnt how to make long voyages out of sight of land (before the compass was known) was shown when, in the first century AD, they started a regular sea trade between the Red Sea ports and the west coast of India. The Arab dhows had long sailed this route, using the south west monsoon for the outward voyage and the north east monsoon winds for the return. But whereas the lightly constructed dhows followed the coast around the

Persian Gulf all the way to India, keeping in touch with the land in the age old tradition of Mediterranean voyaging, the Roman *corbitae* were great strong vessels and they made the voyage direct in both directions. With the gradual decline of the power of Rome, however, this little-known sea trade ceased, and only the Arab dhows continued as they do to this day.

Remarkable though the Romans were in the way they learnt to build big seagoing ships, and in their architectural and engineering feats — the splendid straight paved roads they built over Europe as well as in Britain, their fine arched bridges, impressive buildings, and some stupendous aqueducts spring to mind — I still wonder how their engineers managed to make all the calculations that would be necessary for such works, when one considers the Roman numbering system. Possibly the humble *abacus* (like today's pocket calculators) did all the figuring that must have been necessary.

From out of the mist, a small Roman freighter

My thoughts were still hovering over such events of the past when slowly into view appeared what could have been the mast of a Roman freighter making her way slowly in the calm along the coast. But as it materialised out of the mist it turned out to be the Hook Beacon, standing stark as a warning finger. With its topmark shaped in the form of an inverted cone, it has always reminded me of the stormy day long ago when I cajoled a kindly aunt to let me borrow her umbrella to go to the school sports; and how the thing got blown inside out by a sudden gust, and what a job I had to get it back to look more like its original shape before I handed it back to its innocent owner.

As the morning wore on the sun, like a brazen disc, marched across a cloudless sky, reflecting from the still water until our eyes hurt and we would have sought some shade if there had been any. Pitiless is the sun in countries nearer the Equator where people cover their bodies with clothes to keep off his rays, and houses are built with blind walls and shady inner courtyards, turning their backs on the sun. It is only in our northern climes that men and women claim to be sun-worshippers, and judge the success of their holidays on how much sun they were able to soak up in sun tan. Today, without sunglasses, we were thankful even for the slight easing of the heat that this mist afforded us.

And so our ship drifted in silence, until out of the haze appeared anther seamark, a small conical buoy. I recognised it as the South Spit on the edge of the Margate Hook Sand.

'We haven't a hope now,' I said resignedly, 'of catching our fair tide round the Foreland today. But here, close to the edge of the Hook Sand and well out of the way of any coasters or fishing boats rushing through the Gore Channel, seems to me as good a place as any to drop the hook and wait to see what happens next.'

With her cable stretched to the sluggish tide *Nightfall* swung round to face the way she had come, while her crew busied themselves with a good tea — Bill likes his boiled eggs and toast to fend off the pangs of hunger before suppertime comes round — and allowed both time and tide to take care of themselves. The sand, a cable's length or so distant, was uncovering, and looked almost golden in the evening sunlight, so tempting in fact to explore that we got into the dinghy, taking the chart with us, and rowed ashore.

'It's as hard as the Maplins or the Pye Sands,' my ship-mate remarked as we walked across the tide-rippled surface to the other side of the sand. 'That bank that's showing across a sort of channel over there,' he added holding up the chart, 'I suppose will be the Last, shown here. And beyond it, stretching away into the nor'eastward for five miles or so will be Margate Sand. My goodness, Maurice, what a devilish shoal to have right in the southern approach to the Thames Estuary. There must've been countless wrecks on these sands through the ages.'

'And yet,' I pointed out, 'these same sands not only have proved a graveyard for hundreds of ships, but they can also help to protect vessels when riding out a storm under their lee. I bet there's been many a shipmaster glad of the shelter behind one of these vast shoals in a winter's gale.'

At the time I did not know how prophetic my remark was to prove, but something over eight years later, in the cold December of 1940 when decks had ice on them for weeks on end, I was to recall this very anchorage and to be fully grateful for the comparative shelter that Margate Sand could offer during a northerly blizzard. In command of a small North Sea trawler which was specially equipped for recovering enemy mines, I was ordered from the convoy assembly anchorage off Southend to Dover for a special operation, and as night came on with a half gale from the north I had her Grimsby skipper bring her through the Four Fathom Channel and anchor her almost exactly in *Nightfall's* spot. Here under the lee of the Margate Hook Sands we were able to ride out a truly wintry night in comparative shelter.

Knowing some of these anchorages in the Thames Estuary where an expanse of drying sands can make a very useful harbour with the wind in the right direction — and a dangerous lee shore if it decided to blow in the opposite direction! — has been able to save me many an exhausting slog merely to get into the nearest river with its more familiar anchorages. Although shoals to windward when the tide covers them are naturally not so effective as a firm weather shore, nevertheless even at high water they do calm down the seas to some extent, and to leeward of them there is nothing like the turmoil that you would find on the windward side of the shoal.

As soon as the tide begins to drop sufficiently for only a foot or two to cover the sands to windward, peace seems to come over the sea, and all the viciousness it has out there to windward is calmed down. Sheltering thus under the lee of outlying sands of any estuary is usually peaceful as in any river on an average from about two hours after high water until about two hours before the next high water: in other words, you can generally rely on having up to eight hours of comparative calm at anchor. And if you feel, as many yachtsmen no doubt do, nervous about being caught if the wind switches round while you are getting some sleep, believe me there is no need to worry. Experience has shown that immediately the wind drops, or changes direction, you will be awake in an instant. And provided you have been wise enough to have your sails all ready for hoisting at short notice, the anchorage in the open sea behind a sheltering shoal need be no more risky than any anchorage in a river.

Back on board as the setting sun laid its path across the water and lit up the drying sands with a mellow golden light, Bill and I settled in our corners in the cabin with our feet up and a glass of something soothing in our hands. While he gazed up at the deckhead and his trusty pipe crackled contentedly, I read him extracts from Volume Two of Frank Cowper's *Sailing Tours (Nore to the Scilly Isles)*, which first appeared in 1893. Following in the wake of lone sailing men like Lieut E Middleton, whose *Cruise of the Kate* described a single-handed voyage round England in 1869, H Fiennes Speed (*Cruises in Small Yachts*, 1883) and R T Macmullen (*Down Channel*) who was found dead at the tiller of his yacht by fishermen off the French coast (surely an old warrior's way to go!), Frank Cowper was the first to compose a series of sailing directions for generations of cruising men to come.

Starting from the Thames in the 1880s 'Jack-All-Alone', as he often signed himself, explored all the harbours and rivers of the English coasts, mostly alone and, of course, entirely under sail and sweep. His *Tours* with their neatly drawn coloured charts are still a delight to read, for he was a scholarly man and well versed in the Classics. He spent the last few years of a long life in the Hostel of St Cross at Winchester (he was a Wykehamite), and I recall with pleasure the chat we had about yacht cruising when I called to pay my respects to the old man while he was still alive. It has always seemed to me a pity to wait for a man's funeral before showing one's appreciation of his life's work.

'No place, is there Maurice,' Bill was saying, 'quite like a boat's cabin . . . oh sorry, did I wake you?'

I had indeed nodded off, but my shipmate's remark helped to warm a proud owner's heart, for I thought *Nightfall's* cabin was by far the most pleasing of any boat I had owned to date. It was a pure period piece with its mahogany and beechwood panelling, the skylight over the varnished leaf table, the figured carpet on the floor toning in with the red settee cushions and backrests, and above them the carved rails like miniature bannisters running along the length of the shelves, while mahogany coachroof beams arched darkly against the white deckhead. On the after bulkhead a filigreed brass oil lamp with a mirror reflector gave a soft warm light which was good for reading from an Argand circular wick burner in a tall chimney. That lamp was a particular favourite of mine, for on its base was stamped 'Made in Bavaria', and that placed it, like *Nightfall* herself, before the 1914 War. The evening was too warm for us to have the bogie stove alight, but on a cold night its cheerful glow could turn the whole cabin into the warmest and cosiest place imaginable.

The interiors of small yachts, like contemporary designs in domestic architecture, have come a long way from the traditional pattern of natural wood panelling, corner cupboards with leaded glass-fronted doors, a handsome brass hanging lamp above in the skylight, and the galley discreetly hidden behind the forward bulkhead. And like many of today's glass-walled dwellings and concrete office blocks, many contemporary yachts' interiors appear as cold and stark as a hospital operating theatre.

The present trend of the dinette layout ('converts quickly and easily into a double berth') offers little relaxation to the crew member coming off watch, and wanting only to strip off oilskins and seaboots and just collapse on to a lee settee. The best he can do is to sit up at the dinette table, unless the sea is calm enough for him to retire to one of the bunks forward. But if there is any sea running the motion in the bows of a small yacht can prove disastrous to stomachs and anything but relaxing to the tired hand (or perhaps one should say crew-person).

The popularity of the dinett arrangement, so I am told, is due to demands by owners' wives, not for the benefits of the double bed conversion but because of the extent of the galley opposite, with its lengthy working top, its stainless sink and drainer, cooker with oven, fridge and ample lockers — a housewife's dream. With the kids seated at the table, knives and forks at the ready, Mum has only to turn around to serve the hungry mouths. 'It's always the wife who has the final say in buying a boat,' more than one smart salesman at Boat Shows has told me. 'Women invariably fall for the dinette with galley opposite arrangement, and it's just that which we find sells most of the yachts.'

For the boating family with young children who are necessarily confined to limited day sailing with long periods at anchor close to a beach, or alongside a staging in one of the yacht marinas, it is not disputed that the cabin with dinette layout can be almost ideal. It is when the family are grown up, or there are only adults aboard, and much more extensive cruising is undertaken, that the limitations of the dinette become apparent. After a long day's sail and when all are tired it can be a weary chore to clear the supper table so that the dinette can be rearranged for the two who are just dying to get to bed and sleep. On a long passage with the traditional two-settee berth layout a hand can come below off watch and tumble into the lee berth and get some rest. And if proper bunk dodgers are fitted the settee to windward can be similiarly used for sleep. The conventional seagoing yacht's cabin arrangement was not developed overnight but has stood the test of time, and when the layout is changed to something quite different to suit the needs of today's sailing families, the pros and cons have to be accepted.

The following morning while Bill took a pre-breakfast dip overboard and I volunteered to attend to the bacon and eggs, it became evident that we had to get ashore that day for we were running out of water and stores. The mist of the previous evening had gone, and the horizon glinted like diamonds in the morning sun, but there was only the lightest of breezes from about north east. It was, therefore, a decidedly slow fetch close-hauled along the shoreline past Westgate, and for a time we discussed the possibility of making for the entrance to Margate Harbour.

Neither of us had ever been into the place before, by land or by water, and Bill began to read up what the Sailing Directions had to say of it. 'Listen to this,' he said.

'Craft can only enter the harbour towards high water, and if intending to stay must be prepared to take the mud. There is little shelter, and yachtsmen are not recommended to enter without a special reason.'

By unanimous vote it was decided that our good ship should press on for Ramsgate, which was not many miles away.

Without unduly pinching her — and like most shallow draught yachts *Nightfall* never took kindly in any light head wind to being sailed as close as a Six Metre — we could not weather the ledges off Foreness, for it was apparent that the headland was slowly soaking past to windward of our bowsprit. A short leg seaward away from Palm Bay, however, soon put us in a better position to fetch the Longnose buoy on the next tack, and after the vertical-striped monster had washed slowly past we were relieved to ease sheets a little and creep past the white bluffs of Botany Bay, White Ness and the Foreland itself with the lighthouse and a tall chimney to westward of it dominant against the skyline.

'It's years since I was last in Ramsgate,' Bill remarked as the piers of the harbour began to detach themselves from the background scenery. 'I suppose it'll still have a muddy wall with a long weedy ladder to climb up, shrimp and whelk stalls on the quay, comic postcard kiosks, and trippers in funny hats, as I remember.'

'But,' I said to encourage him, 'we'll be able to get all the stores we want, and we'll only stay just overnight.'

'Aye aye, skipper. And I'll tell you another thing. We'll

find a damn good restaurant in the town and have a slap up meal.' His eyes grew misty with the thought of it. 'I think I rather fancy the idea of a sole meunière with pommes croquettes and fresh garden peas, with rum baba or a chocolate mousse to follow. And washed down with a nicely chilled bottle of Chablis. What'll be your choice, oh skipper?'

I said my first choice right now was a safe berth where we could leave our ship while we were ashore, and we busied ourselves with warps and fenders as we edged our way round the end of the mole and the expanse of harbour opened before us. In slow motion as it were, for here the wind was baffling and unpredictable with occasional sharp little puffs from over the wall, *Nightfall* eased her unhurried way alongside a sizable fishing boat which looked friendly, and came to rest for the time being.

Bill was able to gratify his wishes that evening at the meal I gladly stood him as a good shipmate, except that we had to settle for our soles grilled (the restaurant didn't do meunière), plum pie in place of the rum baba, and a bottle of Graves instead of the Chablis, but the coffee suitably laced was a good punctuation mark. Our enjoyment of high living in one of England's watering places was, however, tempered a little by the news I had received when putting a routine call through to the office: a thing I have often felt one should never do when away on holiday. It appeared there was a crisis brewing and my immediate return was held to be advisable to help deal with it. There was nothing for it, therefore, but I must cut short our little cruise together, put on collar and tie and catch the morning train for London.

For the moment I swore at Alexander Graham Bell and his wonderful invention for catching me in such an unappetising harbour — there was as yet no well-organised yacht basin in Ramsgate — for I should far rather have been at least in the Orwell. But I needn't have fretted. The ever resourceful Bill said not to worry — if I would trust him with *Nightfall* he would call up Martin C, an old friend of Cambridge days, who was always keen to get a sail in anything at any time, and see if he was free to join the ship and help sail her home.

Martin proved only too eager to come for a short dash across the Thames Estuary, and I was able to leave in the morning with the other commuters with the comforting feeling that my ship was in capable hands. And so it was that, after the office problems had been sorted out and routine restored, the next weekend I was able to get down to Pin Mill, *Nightfall* was safely back on a mooring, neatly stowed, even the grime of Ramsgate cleaned off, generally in shipshape condition.

A skipper can owe a great deal to competent and thoughtful shipmates with whom he can entrust his little ship.

Margate Hook Beacon

9

Tides are forces to reckon with

Sailing has been described light-heartedly as the slowest from of transport enjoyed by man. There is more than a grain of truth in this when one considers that the rate of progress over the ground of a small boat under sail, taking light winds and strong, fair winds and foul, and periods of calm into consideration, is likely to average little more than three nautical miles in the hour. A healthy man can walk faster.

This slow average speed of any small wind driven-vessel, by which is meant a boat within the twenty- to thirty-foot range, is a reason why the tides can become such factors in her favour, or enemies to her progress. The wise skipper therefore studies the tidal streams and tide tables relating to his area with great care, so as to make whatever use he can of them. The same importance of working one's tides when bound away on a passage applies with almost equal effect to the small low-powered motor cruiser.

It is natural, pride of ownership being what it is, that many boat owners overestimate the speed at which their boats are going. It behoves an owner to check the speed on his beloved craft once in a while by a stop watch over any measured mile he comes across, or between two points on the chart if he knows the distance: and to allow for the effects of the tide if there is any.

Every vessel, whether small yacht, motor cruiser, square rigger, steam ship, motor ship or what have you, has her own maximum speed which she is unable to exceed. Only unorthodox types, such as catamarans, trimarans, racing dinghies and speedboats, are a law unto themselves once they can get up on the water and plane, and we need not consider their speed capabilities here. For every *conventional* single hull vessel there is a simple yardstick by which her maximum speed attainable under either power or sail is obtained, and it is related to her length on the waterline.

The formula was first introduced by William Froude, a naval architect, scientist, and mathematician, who carried out a series of trials on model ships and yachts in a special test tank during the 1870s. He it was discovered that the speed of any displacement vessel of normal design was directly governed by its waterline length. With sailing vessels — and this included yachts — his tests showed that the maximum speed in knots (nautical miles per hour) of which the vessel was capable under ideal conditions of strong fair wind and smooth seas could be calculated from the square root of the WL in feet mulitplied by a factor of one-point-four. This is assuming a well designed hull with smooth lines and a fine run aft, as in a good yacht.

From this formula, therefore, it can be calculated that a yacht of any good conventional design 36ft on the waterline could reach $(1.4 \sqrt{36}) = 8.4$ knots when sailing in smooth conditions, or a 24-footer $(1.4 \sqrt{24}) = 6.86$ knots. For very short periods, as when a yacht is surfing down the face of a big following sea, the speed might build up to 50% or more of these figures (to the owner's delight), but as she sinks back into the trough her speed through the water might drop to almost zero. In big seas, therefore, the *average* will be well below the Froude figure.

In racing yachts in the past, designers endeavoured to gain as much sailing length as they could by adding a U-sectioned overhang at the bow and a long flat counter stern, so that when heeled the *effective* length of the waterline would be considerably increased, with a corresponding lift in the sailing speed. The once-famous cutter yacht *Satanita** had the longest waterline length of any cutter rigged yacht built, namely 93.5ft (28.5m) with a length on deck of 131.5ft (40.1m). She was exquisitely fine lined and such were her overhangs that, when driven as hard as her spars could stand, her effective sailing length could reach 124ft (38m). This would make it possible for her when sailing on a broad reach

*Designed by J M Soper. His lines may be compared with those of G L Watson's *Britannia* in Uffa Fox's *Sailing, Seamanship and Yacht Construction*, Peter Davies, 1934.

at slack water between the Nab and Owers lightvessels in near gale conditions during the summer of 1893 to have logged 16 knots. This must have been her ultimate sailing speed: any attempt to drive her faster would only have caused her to heel farther over, bury her lee rail with all the drag that implies, and immediately lose speed. Incidentally for the record of days long past, *Satanita's* mainboom was 91ft (27.7m) in length. They were indeed giants in yachting in those days.

The recorded speeds of 16, 17 and 18 knots claimed by some of the more celebrated tea clippers of the 1860s (*Cutty Sark, Thermopylae, Lightning* et al) when they were racing home to catch the best of the London tea markets, hardly compared with the performance just noticed. But *Satanita* was a racing yacht with a particularly beautiful slimlined hull, while the clipper ships, fine lined though they were compared with contemporary merchant vessels, were first and foremost dividend earning cargo carriers, although only a lightweight cargo. Whilst the best of them were known to have reeled off sixteen to eighteen seamiles in the hour when running before strong winds with every square yard of canvas their spars would carry, sometimes overtaking steamships in these stirring conditions, their performance fell well below Froude's $1.4 \sqrt{WL}$ formula.

In speed trials under sail today we have seen specially built racing trimarans and other multi-hull conceptions achieving velocities far in excess of this, while racing planing dinghies commonly break through Froude's displacement speed/length formula as if it were an aquatic sound barrier. Today's speedboats, skittering along the surface like teatrays down the stairs (and even more bumpy!) take no notice of the limits of an ordinary displacement craft; but it is a sobering thought on the resistance water has on any moving hull, that even the giant liner 900ft on the waterline attempting the old Blue Riband of the Atlantic with her 34 knots is putting up a speed/length ratio of only $1.13 \sqrt{WL}$, while most ocean going vessels run at an economical speed well below that given by the formula.

Descending, as it were, from flights of fancy amongst the clouds to the more mundane world of ordinary little cruising yachts groping their way around our coasts, we are forced to appreciate how important are the tidal streams to our rate of progress. If we consider that our little ship of, say, 24ft WL cannot under any conditions sail in smooth water at more than 7 knots (6.86 by Froude's formula), it is reasonable to suppose that for most of the time when cruising our speed will be in the four- to five-knot bracket.

Now if the tide in our area runs at, say, 2½ knots we can therefore make between 6½ and 7½ knots with it over the ground. But if the same tide is against us our rate over the ground will have dropped to a measly 1½ to 2½ knots. This assumes a fair, or commanding, breeze; but if we are compelled to beat against a head wind then the difference between progress on each tack and barely holding our own becomes even more vital.

The motto which I have long carried in the various boats I have owned, 'Make the Tides your Friends', should therefore be taken to heart by all skippers and navigators of small cruising yachts and low speed motor cruisers. From my house at West Mersea which overlooks the mouth of the Blackwater I sometimes see little white plastic sloops, perhaps with dad and mum and two smaller figures clothed suitably as the advertisements advise in bright orange and blue waterproofs, leaving bound, they said, for Harwich and the Orwell, when the north-going ebb has already been running three hours or more. And it brings a sadness to think what they are quite likely running themselves and their children into: the tide turning foul between Clacton and Frinton, the easterly wind perhaps breezing up, and the evening coming on.

If the effect of a two-knot tide can be so important to a little yacht, how much more serious can be a really strong tide, such as is to be met in our River Humber, and in many other places. The implacable power of a volume of water moving in a great stream has to be experienced to be believed. Water is essentially heavy stuff, for a cubic foot of sea water weighs 64 pounds (29 kg), and a tidal stream carries thousands of tons along with it.

Strong tides, of five knots or more, can be highly dangerous to small craft, and have to be treated with care. Not many years ago one of the powerful Hull steam trawlers backed out from Kingston dock into a spring ebb. She carried her way a little too far and, before her engines could get her going ahead, she dug her stern into a shoal almost opposite the dock entrance. The tide immediately caught hold of her, rolled her down until she lay on her beam ends, carrying two of her crew overboard, and almost buried her in the mud.

The Hooghly is notorious for the strength of the currents that pour down this great winding river past Calcutta into the Bay of Bengal. In sailing ship days when there was no commanding breeze from the north, vessels had to be worked down using their anchors on a short cable so as to hold the vessel's head to the current, as the Thames spritty used her anchor to drudge down river in a calm. The art is to keep the anchor dragging, or drudging, over the bottom while the stream flows past the hull and gives the necessary pressure on the rudder to maintain steerage way.

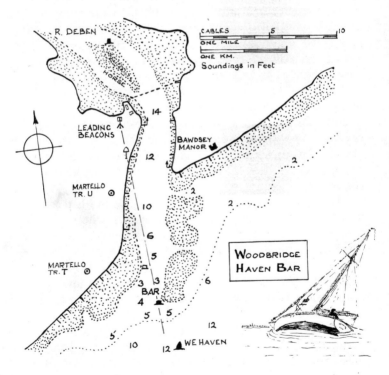

On the bar in a calm

Disasters on the Hooghly were common enough, and even in steamship days when the pilots could bring their vessels down using the engines, a sudden manoeuvre to avoid another vessel, a misjudgement on the part of the pilot, a fault in the steering gear, or even temporary engine failure, could result in a grounding on one of the banks before the anchor could be let go and holding. When such a thing happened the current, running at six knots or more, would have the power to force the ship round broadside on and roll her right over. The Hooghly has claimed many ship disasters over the years.

Just how this could happen, but in only a minor way, was shown to me in a sharp lesson I had on a calm evening in late summer some years before the War. I had completed almost two enjoyable seasons of weekend sailing up and down the East Coast in my 9.5m cutter *Nightfall* without an engine. But after being becalmed all one misty day outside the Goodwins, being carried northward on the ebb through some awkward overfalls, and then ignominiously back through the same stretch of angry water on the evening flood, while ships' syrens blared all round us, I had succumbed to the convenience of an 'iron topsail'.

This had taken the form of a converted car engine taken out of a wrecked Bullnose Morris 11.9 two-seater, and was lined up to the shaft and propeller belonging to the original slow-running two-stroke engine. But this screw proved too coarse of pitch for the car engine which could not reach its higher revs to give *Nightfall* more than 4½ knots with full throttle.

It was a Sunday afternoon at Pin Mill, and I had arranged to take my boat round to Woodbridge, where the yard promised to have her hauled out and a more efficient screw fitted before the following weekend. (Later, after this had been done, the same engine gave *Nightfall* a lively 6½ knots — a fifty per cent increase in speed — clearly showing how important it is to find the right diameter, pitch and type of propeller to suit both the engine and the boat.)

I was on my own, having come down from London by train, and was keen to catch the evening train back from Woodbridge, and in warm sunshine and a calm that inverted the trees on both banks on to the mirror-like surface of the river, we motored quietly down on the ebb. I was reckoning to time my arrival off the mouth of the Deben just after low water so as to be able to take the first of the flood up the river to Woodbridge.

It was a lovely day, and I was thinking as the fields and woods passed on each side how fortunate we sailing men were in these parts to have two of the prettiest rivers in the East of England within a few miles of each other, not to mention the broad Stour leading up to Mistley from the very mouth of the Orwell, even though the channel beyond Wrabness was narrow and winding. Then round the corner, so to speak, a few miles beyond Dovercourt were the extensive creeks and islands of Walton Backwaters where, in those days, you could find a deserted anchorage for every evening of the week. All this within a radius of an hour or so's sailing.

While I sat musing at the tiller, the entrance to Felixstowe Dock opened out as it passed by to port, and I was pleased to note the sprits of two barges against the dark red brick face of Marriage's mills. This, remember, was the summer of 1933 and for long Felixstowe Dock had been almost deserted and derelict, so that it was rare to see a steam coaster or even barges at its quays. This seemed a sad end to the high hopes of its originator, the irascible Colonel Tomline of Orwell Park, who had engineered and built in the 1870s the Felixstowe Railway which led off the Great Eastern's line at Westerfield Junction to his new dock facing across the harbour to the town of Harwich. Little did one imagine then how this sleepy dock and its surrounding wasteland would develop in the 1970s and become, in conjunction with Ipswich and Parkstone Quay, the largest and busiest dock complex in the East of England.

A mile farther on, the same shore was dominated by the great black hangars used by the flying boats as their Felixstowe base. One of these handsome aircraft was riding to her mooring buoy just out of the main ship channel, and as I steered *Nightfall* close past one could get an impression of her size. With the four airscrews now still she sat the water as graceful as a gull with something like a thirty-metre wing span and some eight metres from the waterline to the top of the flight deck. But the short-lived era of the giant passenger carrying flying boat, with its lush cabins and staircases and near silence in flight, was already over. These ships of the air required up to three miles of open smooth water to take off when fully laden, while the even bigger American Clipper flying boats needed five miles. There were few such stretches of water throughout the world which could be kept clear for flying boats alone and, just as they had ousted the great disaster-prone Zeppelin-type dirigible airships in their day, so they were soon to be displaced on the world's air routes by the forthcoming jet airliner. I was lucky enough in 1941 to be flown form Cairo across Central Africa to Lagos in one of the last of the Sunderlands, and thence to the UK in the giant American Clipper — a fascinating experience for an RNVR bloke after a spell of enemy mine clearance in the Suez Canal.

It may have been that I had underestimated the strength of the ebb which had carried us down the Orwell, round the Landguard Point and the Platters shoals, and along past the crowds on the beach at Felixstowe; or perhaps *Nightfall*'s engine was doing a little better than I had realized, but as the first of the two Martello towers at Felixstowe Ferry drew abeam and I could note the tide still washing northward past the black Haven buoy, it was evident that this ebb was not quite done. Should I stop the engine, I wondered, drop the hook and wait for the first of the flood? But the thought that I had that train to catch spurred me on. I knew that with a spring tide like this one at mid ebb the stream poured out between the banks of shingle at some five to six knots, but it must be within half an hour of low water, and I reasoned that the worst of the stream must be over by now. Also, from previous soundings when going over the bar, I calculated there ought to be just about four feet at the shallowest part beyond the buoy. With *Nightfall*'s draught of 3ft 3in I decided there should be enough to get over.

With the sea like a mirror in the haze, and with only a slight swell coming in to cause the shingle banks on each side of the bar to murmur like bursts of clapping on the radio (how different from the angry roar of this place when there was a fresh onshore breeze blowing!) I steered *Nightfall* up to the little black barrel buoy and looked for the two leading marks amongst the houses at the Ferry.

Sitting relaxed with my right arm over the tiller I saw that we were only just creeping up against the tide: it was still flowing out faster than I had expected, and although I opened the throttle wide, the engine, gamely thumping its oversize propeller round, was making painfully slow progress over the ground. I had perhaps forgotten how any boat under power draws her stern down, and further, how this effect can be aggravated while she is in shallow water and the keel 'smells the bottom'. I should have considered that in these very conditions *Nightfall* as she struggled along was probably drawing as much as four feet.

In an attempt to get out of the worst of the stream I tried edging her gently over towards the shingle bank on the north side, still determined to get into the river if I could. It was a mistake. Before I could correct it the current had caught her bow, she slewed round to starboard, and I felt her keel shudder as it grated on the bottom.

Immediately the tiller slammed over against the coaming with the press of water against the rudder, and I found myself helplessly pinned in the corner of the cockpit. In an agonising movement poor old *Nightfall* lurched over until her lee deck was under and the water poured round her bow and stern and lapped close to the top of the cockpit coaming. My God, MG, I couldn't help thinking, you've done all the wrong things and you've bloody well asked for it. There've been scores of vessels of all kinds lost on this bar, so you can't claim to be the first by a long chalk!

For some moments I was winded, and could not move from the tiller's vice-like grip, while the engine, with its propeller churning in aerated water, was racing like a mad thing and scattering a cloud of spray from under the counter. While I pushed and struggled to free myself the boat seemed to teeter on the turn of her bilge, grinding ominously over the gravel bottom, and the stories of ships in the Hooghly being rolled right over and their crews drowned, flashed through my mind. My heart ached for the good little ship which had obeyed my hand on her tiller, and always done all I had ever asked of her, and I felt ashamed that I should have brought her into this mess.

At last I managed to climb upwards and free myself, switch off the crazy engine, and in the ensuing peace but for

the steady rush of the water I crouched in the cockpit waiting
to see what would happen next. Slowly, oh so slowly, the force
of the current became a little less, and my brave boat took on a
more solid feeling as though she had come to terms with the
situation (more adequately than her master) and would not go
over any further.

It gave a chance to light the primus and brew up some tea
and take stock, for it was by now well after the time of low
water and the level of the water had begun rise. Soon the out-
flow was held back and the blessed flood tide began to trickle
slowly inward. *Nightfall* stirred herself, came up on to an even
keel, and began little scrapes along the gravel bed as the tide
caressed her hull.

The engine sprang into life, the clutch was let in, and lo!
she was once again heading past the now silent shingle and the
many-towered red brick pile of Bawdsey Manor on the north
cliff, eager once again to carry the young flood up the winding
reaches of the lovely little Deben.

Wet evening at the Rock, River Deben

It had been a subduing reminder not to try to enter a river with a bar like that at the wrong state of the tide, even in a flat calm. I thought — hoped — I had learnt the lesson this time, and when we reached the old world quay at Woodbridge I hardly felt I deserved the willing help and courtesy of the yard proprietor on this Sunday evening as he took *Nightfall* off my hands, promising to have her out of the water and the new propeller fitted next day, so as to have her ready for the following weekend.

With hurried thanks I almost ran to the charmingly situated station, which looks straight down the prettily wooded river, just in time to catch the crowded train for Liverpool Street. A chastened and somewhat thoughtful skipper, I felt the sea had shown me in no uncertain terms that she would allow no man to take liberties with her, even when she pretended to be in one of her calmest moods.

10

Two ways across the estuary

Strong winds had heralded almost a fortnight of bad weather as one depression followed another across the country. With them had come rain storms, flooded fields and washed out holidays, from which many families, wearing the resigned look of the British on holiday, returned home early. Amongst them was my old shipmate, DJ, who had been forced to leave his yawl *Signora* at Ostende, like a number of other yachts homeward bound, and had come home ignominiously on the packetboat so as not to be late at his office. Now the BBC weathermen were forecasting a spell of finer weather for the next few days with 'winds south to south west, moderate,' and Duncan was on the line to my office.

'Could you take a couple of days off, old boy,' he was saying, 'to help me get the old hooker back to Heybridge? I hate having to leave her in that smelly harbour.' His familiar chuckle was clear enough on the telephone. 'It looks as if we'll have just the conditions I've been waiting for, and we could catch tonight's boat, if you can manage it.'

It was always a pleasing experience — and often educational — to sail with D, and when we boarded his ship next morning in the harbour at Ostende it began to look as though the Met men had got it right this time, for the wind was indeed between south and south-west and just a nice whole sail breeze. My friend's *Signora* was of the old school, a straight stemmer with a square counter stern, some 10m long on deck, and somewhat narrow gutted with a long bowsprit, a deep forefoot and a long straignt iron keel. She was heavily rigged with gaff mainsail and a small gaff mizzen perched close to the taffrail: in short, a homely old cruising yacht typical of 1890 when she had been built.

She was not the only English yacht to be cooped up in the harbour by the strong winds of the previous two weeks, and we found that two of the other 'foreign' boats had crews on board who were rarin' to make a dash of it back to England on this tide. One of these was a powerful and handsome gaff cutter of about 11m, with a transom stern, while the other was a more modern Bermudian sloop with a fair overhang at bow and stern and a sleek look about her. The cutter, her owner told us, was bound home to Pin Mill, while the sloop was making for West Mersea. Anxious as we all were to get back home before any more bad weather came along, they had already started up their engines and the dockside reverberated with the murmur of their exhausts.

'They'll be nice to have in company,' said D as we singled up our warps, 'for some of the way, at least. I'll get the BB started.'

Signora's engine held us both in a sort of love-hate relationship. It was a massive single cylinder two-stroke (but it ran so unevenly that I sometimes doubted if it could count even up to two) and I am sure that it ought to have been put in a museum. The manufacturers, D told me, proudly described it as a Belfast Barker, which on occasion we translated in our own idiom, and it was supposed to date from 1908. Like a rusty Iron Maiden, its tall cylinder glowered in the shadows behind the cabin steps, and when it was running, thumping like a mill engine, a fixed brass starting handle on the rim of the big open flywheel whirled round like a golden St Catherine wheel, just feeling for trouser turnups. Old time steam engine practice was reflected in the brass sight-feed lubricator (I don't think petroil mixture for two-strokes had been introduced in 1908) and in the eccentric rod which worked up and down behind the flywheel operating a device on the front of the cylinder (the 'make-and-break') which produced the spark from a dry accumulator. D had had the monster overhauled and cured of some of its worst habits since I had first sailed with him, and it was thumping away quite happily now as we followed the other two yachts between the long piers out to the harbour entrance.

'The weather forecast,' D remarked as our bowsprit first began to curtsy to the swell coming in, 'said this depression is passing over to the east'ard, and the wind will veer more to the nor'westerly. That makes sense, as the glass has risen a couple of tenths.' He sniffed the breeze, which brought with it a pungent variety of smells from the town we were leaving that would have entranced any dog, and looked again at his chart of the Southern North Sea.

'Our direct course for home,' he said, 'is just about nor'west for the Galloper and the Longsand Head — what's that now, say sixty miles — and then about west-nor'west for the Goldmer Gat at the end of the Gunfleet Sand, and home through the Wallet. But I don't think it's going to pay us to go that way.'

I knew better than to query my skipper's judgement, for he had many more years' experience of cruising than I had and knew all the tricks. Besides, I was determined for this passage to be the model crew, to be ever willing, prompt in getting meals, never to be seasick and useless, and certainly never to argue. Just how long I could last in that state of saintliness I couldn't tell, and from my look of doubt as I thought over it my skipper must have inferred that I was querying his tactics.

'This wind is almost bound to fetch up in the nor'west,' he explained. 'When, we can't say, but most likely with this glass rising as it is it would catch us long before we got to the Galloper. Then we'd have a dead noser all the way to the Goldmer Gat, and without any shelter from the coast or any of the sands.'

'Then, what will be our course from here? Tell me, oh wise man of the sea, and I will hold her to it like a bloodhound on the scent.'

'I propose we lay this course,' he replied, running a finger across the chart. 'Ostende piers to the Princess Channel is shown as W by N¾N, distance 66 miles. If we're lucky and hold our wind sou'westerly — no worse than that — and can fetch it on one tack before it begins to veer to the nor'west we ought to be in a better position to bear away a little to cross the Barrow. If the wind does fly into the nor'west and breezes up, as well it might, we should at least be in more sheltered waters than out there between the Galloper and the Sunk, shouldn't we?'

117

Old One Lung had ceased his rhythmic thumping and was now cooling off below in a sultry mist, while our sails — jib, staysail, mainsail and mizzen — were set and drawing well as I held the yawl on the course D had given me, while the ends of Ostende piers dropped steadily astern. Our little ship had come into her own again, doubtless as glad as we were to have left the harbour which was, even in those days, already showing all the signs of becoming like an extension of Southend High Street. She leant over to the sou'westerly just forward of our beam and smashed her way through the short chop with powerful thrusts. There is something very comforting, yet difficult to define, about the feel of an old time yacht which, like a smack, is long on the keel, strong and heavy, and resolute in keeping to her course, with none of that tendency of many contemporary yachts to yaw wildly and cry for control by the helmsman every yard of the way. *Signora* seemed to know where she was going, and I thoroughly enjoyed my three hour trick with the tiller tucked under my right arm and feet braced against the lee side of the cockpit. And *Signora*'s cockpit was deep and comfortable; it was not one of those shallow self-drainers, and I never heard that any water, bar rain and spray, ever tumbled into it.

The skipper's ruddy face appeared through the hatchway beaming with pleasure as he handed out mugs of coffee.

'Boy, oh boy,' he exclaimed, 'this is the life. Better than bending over an office desk all day long, isn't it? Better, too, than that godawful passage we made together bringing the old girl home from Flushing, when we were both as sick as cats. D'you remember that?'

Did I not. That had been my first experience of a real gale in a little yacht at sea, and long afterwards I wrote a yarn about it.* Through the binoculars D was watching the two yachts which had left the harbour ahead of us. They were already some distance away on our lee beam, both apparently keeping on a nor'westerly course.

'I can understand the cutter heading up for the Galloper,' he remarked, 'for she's going for Harwich and Pin Mill. She's got no option. But the owner of that white sloop told me they were heading for West Mersea, and he'd also heard the same weather forecast. He's evidently decided to keep company

Swatchways and Little Ships

with the cutter and part somewhere near the Longsand Head. They know we're bound for the Blackwater, too, and I shouldn't be surprised if they're wondering right now where the deuce we think we're going!'

Visibility was good, and until the land to windward gradually dropped below the horizon the line of low cliffs between Ostende and Nieupoort, with here and there a water tower, was etched clearly against the afternoon sky. Away from the coast the sea was a soft green, flecked in places with flashes of white as a wave broke, and we enjoyed the sight of four or five of those powerful-looking trawlers from Ostende with their high rusty bows and stumpy masts fishing further inshore. Along this coast the line of extensive banks — the Wenduyne, the Stroom, the Nieupoort, the Small — undoubtedly affords some protection to small craft keeping inside them when bound up and down the coast. In thick weather a yacht, so as to avoid being run down by a ship in the main channel, might anchor right over one of these banks, provided the skipper chooses a place with sufficient water at low tide. But if he feels safe enough from the bigger ships and coasters, he should bear in mind that the local fishing boats sometimes cut across these banks where there is enough water, without expecting to find a foreign yacht anchored there. An anchor watch, with bell or foghorn, is a proper precaution, therefore, until the fog lifts.

'...they're wondering right now where the deuce we think we are going!'

Some miles away to leeward the masts of the West Hinder stuck out of the sea like exclamation marks, the hull itself below the horizon, as the lightvessel drew abeam and steadily dropped astern. And as the afternoon wore on the wind began to harden a little, and every now and then a heavier puff would have *Signora* heeling almost down to the coveringboard, and bustling along like an elderly lady hurrying for a train.

Darkness spread over the sea to the familiar accompaniment of the creaking gaff jaws, the steady flutter from the leech of the mizzen (we could never cure that; the sail had become too badly stretched over the years) and the rhythmic scend and wash of the seas. Down in the galley, heating up a good thick stew for our supper, I heard my skipper's voice at the helm, his words sounding far away and echoless as voices on deck do to those below.

'Before you get the meal ready, old man,' he called, 'would you help me by stowing the mizzen? The old girl's beginning to pull my arm out.'

Signora was certainly heeling down to the rail now, and while I muzzled the flogging mizzen I realized how the breeze had begun to pipe up since I had gone below to light the primus.

'I think we'll tuck a reef in the main as well, now you're on deck.'

The skipper hauled the staysail sheet a-weather and put the tiller down steadily, securing it with one of the slip lines. Taking her time about it, as any Victorian dame would, *Signora* rounded up almost into the wind with her long bowsprit lifting and falling over the wavecrests, then payed off a little until she was riding quietly, curtsying to the weather. While she lay thus hove-to D and I quickly tucked the first reef in the mainsail. Then we let the staysail flog over to leeward, released the tiller, and with sheets hauled in again the old yawl, under easier canvas, was on her way again; and soon bowls of a belly-warming supper were being served in the lee of the cockpit, while the knowing old hooker sailed her course with tiller again lashed, a little a-weather this time.

It is this faculty to lie quietly when hove-to, and to keep sailing on a more or less straight course unattended with the wind from the weather bow to somewhere abaft the beam, that used to be one of the most endearing qualities of the old-fashioned yacht and fishing smack with long keel and rounded forefoot. It made you feel that you could leave her to take care of you when you were cold and seasick, and probably very frightened as well; it was, I imagine, something akin to the sense of security the driver of a vintage car would feel, aware of the strength of the frame and the chassis around him compared with the tinfoil moulding of present day cars. But like the relative performance of the vintage and the contemporary car, the old time sailing yacht would show up poorly in any race against today's fin-and-skeg highly-tuned racing machines. And if the current trend in yachts results in a boat that will not stay on course herself, but needs constant control by the helmsman, even this exhausting chore — and it can exhaust an entire crew on a long passage in tough weather — can be assuaged by modern science in the form of electric or wind vane self-steering devices. The choice is essentially a personal one: you either like sailing aboard an old timer or driving a vintage car, or you are devoted to the modern fast sloop or Formula One racing car.

When after a few hours with my head down on the lee settee I emerged into the cockpit to take over my next trick at the helm, the dark oilskinned figure of the skipper pointed to windward.

'There's the North Foreland light,' he said, 'just come up over the horizon. It's a helluva powerful light, isn't it? Five flashes every twenty seconds. You should sight the double flash of the NE Spit buoy fine on our weather bow before long. I'll get some shuteye before we get mixed up with the shipping going through the Edinburgh Channel and start sand dodging. Call me, though, if it breezes up any more.'

Signora was still sailing fast through the night, her reefed mainsail stretched pale against the cloudy sky and the foam from her lee bow wave rushing past, hissing as it lipped into the scuppers. The straining jib was tinged at its leech with green from the starboard light, while every now and then, as the yacht lifted over a sea and her powerful bow burst the crest into spray to windward, it caught the red rays of the port lamp. This, I felt, was sailing at its finest with the old yacht straining at the leash, as it were, and determined to take us home as quickly as she was able.

Through the lee rigging the red and white double flash of the Tongue lightvessel came up over the wave tops and steadily passed abeam, while ahead of us the horizon became dotted with so many lights of ships and winking channel buoys that one could imagine we were sailing towards a town, so impressive was the concentration of shipping through this main neck into the Thames Estuary. With no moon, and only a few stars appearing here and there between the clouds, it was too dark to make out any of the forms of the ships that lurked behind their lights. The wind was too boisterous, the seas making too much noise, for one to hear any of their engines as, beneath each group of lights, a totally anonymous vessel slipped past without giving a clue to what she might be — collier, freighter, small tanker or tramp.

We were just able to lay close-hauled through the Edinburgh and had brought the lightvessel close to leeward of us, when there was a sudden lull in the wind, and the jib gave a single shake. For perhaps a minute the breeze appeared to waver, while the washing sound of the waves all around suddenly became loud in one's ears, as though waiting for what next might happen. Then, without warning, the wind was right ahead, coming at us straight out of the north-west. While our jib shook a few times I bore away and *Signora* leant over once more, heading a little east of north, while I looked anxiously astern at two sets of steamers' lights which were following and overtaking fast.

There was no need to call the skipper at this change of conditions, for he had already erupted out of the cabin, pulling on his oilskins, and sized up the situation at a glance.

'Keep her as she is, old man,' he said in unhurried tones, 'and these two ships will pass under our stern. As soon as we're well clear we'll heave-to and put another reef in the main, and I'll get the stays'l off her. It's breezing up quite a bit, isn't it?'

How right the skipper had been, I thought as a few minutes later we tucked in the second reef, in his prophesy of a shift of wind to north west. Here it was on us with a vengeance, and when I got back to the helm and we were underway again, slashing into the steep angry seas, I began to feel glad that we didn't have far to go to get across the Black Deep into Barrow Deep and so get some shelter from the Barrow Sands to windward. Although the wind was already whipping up some nasty short and breaking seas, *Signora* knew how to deal with them, and it was only occasionally that a cloud of spray would lift away from the weather bow, and become suffused with the red glare of the sidelight as it drove aft to embrace the helmsman.

Short tacking through the Barrow Swatch, with the lead going regularly, for it was nearly low water by now, we were able to ease sheets a little and point for the Swin Middle light, while the wind, if anything, blew harder and colder, and we were glad to be under easy canvas. But not far to windward of us now were the Foulness Sands, and the seas no longer had any weight in them, only that moist spitefulness estuary seas can show when infuriated by a wind of Force 6 and a little more.

Dawn was not far off, and when its paler tints began to spread over the sky it etched the blackness of the sea with its growing light, until the upper rim of the sun itself tipped the horizon, separating the breaking crests from the dark hollows between them. As the yellow sun rose it immediately hid behind a dark cloud hovering above the horizon, and the whole sky appeared to take up the promise of wind, more more wind.

But we didn't care, for we were now in familiar home waters with sands and shoals to windward of us, and our little ship, under her double reefed mainsail and jib, was rushing towards the Swin Spitway buoy and taking hardly any notice of the young flood which had turned against her. Close-hauled again, she lay nicely through the Spitway with the tide now under her lee bow, and while the skipper and I settled down in the shelter of the deep cockpit for an early bacon and egg breakfast (Brekka Number One, we called it) *Signora* looked after herself with tiller lashed on the beat up past the Knoll, Colne mouth and Bench Head, while the cold nor'wester seemed to blow great guns until the surface of the Blackwater ahead appeared covered in white tracery.

The skipper's expression as a forkful of egg-bacon was blown away before he could get it into his mouth made me howl with laughter, until the coffee in my mug as I tried to drink it was whipped round my ear by the wind. Maybe, we said, we ought to have hove-to and had breakfast in civilised fashion in the cabin, but worse things can happen at sea.

Later in the forenoon on the tide we stowed our salt-encrusted sails and entered the Heybridge lock. The sky had cleared and groups of small clouds were racing across the blue with all the brightness of a strong north-westerly wind. But on the calm water of the Canal all seemed peace and quiet, and with the warmth of the breeze across the land came the homely scents of hedgerows and grass and tilled fields. We felt we really had come home.

'Well,' remarked my skipper modestly as we put on the sail cover, 'I suppose you could say that our gamble on the weather paid off. I wonder how our two friends got on last night.'

We learnt only many weeks later when we met the owner of the smart little sloop on the hard at West Mersea. He told us that the larger boat, the gaff cutter from Pin Mill, had pulled out ahead of them and been lost sight of soon after they dropped the West Hinder astern. Before they in the sloop sighted the Galloper light, however, he said the wind had flown into the north west and blew hard and dead in their teeth all the way to the Longsand Head and the NE Gunfleet. After putting six rolls in the main and changing to No 2 jib, he told us, they had a very hard thresh against, he reckoned, Force 7 and big awkward seas, so that all three of them aboard were sick and almost exhausted. At one time they thought of trying to lay up into Harwich, to get some shelter and rest, but decided to carry on through the Wallet. The tide, however, turned against them off Clacton and they had a weary slog against it all the way up to West Mersea, picking up their mooring, as far as we could tell, some thirteen hours after *Signora* had locked into Heybridge Basin.

'Funny thing is,' said D after we heard this tale of woe and were looking over the chart again, 'the distance we took through the Edinburgh and the Swin and Spitway is very nearly the same as the route they took by way of Longsand Head and the N E Gunfleet, something like 98 miles. But while the wind was kind to us as soon as we'd got through the

Edinburgh Channel, for them it blew right in their teeth early on. I can well believe him,' he added with his characteristic chuckle, 'when he said there was a bad sea running out by the Galloper.'

Thinking over our forced passage for some time afterwards I came to realize what a lot there is to learn about winds and tides, and how they might be used on occasion to one's advantage. I did feel that my wise old shipmate should be given full credit for knowing so many tricks of cruising in a small yacht on the East Coast.

11

If we are where we think . . .

Although commercial vessels like smacks, barges and coasters have to earn their owners a living and are consequently bound to carry on their work all the year round, February is not a month when you would normally expect to see yachts sailing round the coast. At least, it wasn't in those days. But circumstances made this trip something of a forced passage although happily not a very long one.

Greg had bought a boat which was lying up the Medway at Upnor, and as his home was near Chelmsford he decided that she was too far away across the other side of the Thames for him to be able to start on all the work he wanted to do to her. The sooner he could get the boat to Burnham, where his mooring was, therefore, the sooner he could get on with all the jobs of fitting-out.

He and his sailing partner, Jack, had found the ideal boat in the *Otter*, he explained, through an advertisement in one of the yachting weeklies, and they had at once fallen in love with her. She was cutter rigged, he told me, and although not exactly a new boat her forty years sat lightly upon her because she had been built at a West Country yard where they were used to building those fine Falmouth quay punts, while her accommodation, he assured me, was really sumptuous.

At his suggestion I met Greg and Jack over a sandwich lunch in a Fleet Street wine bar. Greg, fortyish, a keen cruising man with a job in a firm of shipbrokers in the City, and Jack, a little younger, and something in advertising, struck me as a good pair to have as shipmates for they were both of the solid, unflappable kind. The older man made the proposed trip sound very enticing as he described their new purchase.

'It's not far from the Medway round the Whitaker to the Crouch, when you come to think of it,' he said in his deep reassuring voice, 'not for a powerful and fast old hooker like the *Otter*. Given even a bit of a fair slant,' he added as he topped up the glasses again, 'we ought to make it in daylight, easily.'

It could have been the warmth of the bar, in which to Greg's satisfaction women were not allowed, or perhaps the memory of the tedious weeks of winter which had already dragged by without even a chance of stepping aboard a boat, or even the longing one has for a sight of the sea and the sound of the gulls crying on the wind; whatever it was I did not need much pressing to join ship for the trip. When Greg mentioned that it would be something of a luxury cruise, with a fine coal stove in the cabin, a useful small auxiliary engine, and a galley that any cook would be proud to work in, he knew he had me hooked. 'And I hope, old man,' he added with consummate appeal, 'you won't mind doing some of the cooking?'

Some of the . . . ? Ah, that was the purpose of this meeting, for neither of these chaps, I knew, liked to cook and on their own lived on bread and cheese and baked beans; whereas I rather enjoyed working in the galley as Jack with his mechanical flair was happy working under an engine box. I said I'd come if only to see that the partners were properly fed, and accordingly it was agreed we should all three travel down to Rochester by train the following Friday evening, for the morning and evening tides would serve us well.

The late owner, as arranged, had put *Otter* on to a mooring off the Hard at Upnor, and as we rowed out to her with our kitbags on our knees I had to admit she appeared a big and powerful old cutter with the look of a West-countryman, even to the short iron bumkin beside the long bowsprit carrying the forestay some way forward of the straight stem. Some 38ft (11.6 metres) overall, with almost no overhangs, Greg told me, she was of some 16 tons by Thames Measurement, and drew six and a half feet (2.0 metres). This last I took with a pinch of salt, and thought it better, without any comment, to treat it as a good seven feet for navigation purposes.

It was not being cussed, for nearly every cruising yacht I had come across drew more water than her owner believed she did. It was due to a habit most old yachts had of sinking ever deeper after many years of soaking up water, and of having more gear, equipment, fittings, gadgets and stores added to them, and rarely anything taken off; and a check with a tape measure when the vessel was on a hard or hauled out, and the actual float line could be noted on the hull, was the only way to record the true draught when afloat. And even that could become several inches more when the yacht is under power.

Our proud owners had not exaggerated the sense of space below decks, and we all admired the old-fashioned layout where nearly vertical companion steps amidships led down into a panelled saloon with its two settee berths, weighted swing table, glass-fronted corner cupboards, and plenty of standing headroom under the deck beams. To one side of the ladder aft was a small discreet compartment behind a mahogany door — the heads — with opposite a pocketed locker for signal flags above the box housing the four-cylinder Ailsa Craig motor. Beyond this again a panelled door led into a small stateroom with a skylight, two bunks behind curtains with a little dressing table and mirror between them, and a compact wardrobe: the Ladies' Cabin, as it would be marked on the original plans. This must have been a charming arrangement for the occasional Victorian mixed — but entirely respectable — party, with the smoky galley hidden forward of the mast where the paid hand wouldf do all the cooking and sleep in his pipecot in the fo'c's'le: my domain, in fact, for this trip.

At first an all-pervading smell enveloped us of damp bedding, wet sails, tarred rope, paraffin, dead stove ashes, trapped air and rusty bilge water. But after stowing our gear Greg's first action was to light the handsomely decorated iron stove in the saloon while, as ship's cook, I disappeared forward to clean up the galley (two primus stoves clamped to a swinging platform, and the usual cupboards of pots, pans, assorted crockery and breadcrumbs) before serving drinks and preparing a substantial hot supper.

Soon, with doors to all lockers and the cabin opened and

the settee mattresses upended, the heat from the cheerfully roaring stove began to feel its way throughout the ship, drying the bedding and dispelling the musty air of unventilated places. Before the meal was eaten and my shipmates lit up their pipes we had peeled off one outer garment after another until we looked like a promising strip poker team, except that instead of keen poker faces our expressions bore the mark of complete somnolence.

'If this breeze holds like this in the nor'west,' said Greg after he had poked his head out of the hatch, 'we ought to be able to lay nicely across the Estuary and fetch along the edge of the Maplins under their lee.'

'Won't it mean an early start,' asked Jack, 'with high water around six-thirty?'

'I'd like to be underway just before high water,' said our skipper, 'before the old girl starts turning with the tide. Better set the alarm for five o'clock, agreed? We can slip the mooring head to wind and motor down the first reach.'

The decks and cabin top were white with frost when we turned out into the darkness of the early morning and prepared to get underway. The slipperiness of the deck planks did not worry us, however, as the old-fashioned *Otter* had sensible bulwarks almost knee high around her, and they gave one a good feeling of security. Across the water the lights of Chatham Dockyard forestalled the dawn which would soon be taking over the night sky, and there was a bite in the wind that made us beat our hands together and reminded us that this was still winter.

'The wind, bust it,' said our skipper resignedly, 'has gone into the the north during the night. I think it'll pay us to start the engine, Jack, and motor down the river until we are able to lay our course. We can have breakfast on the way.'

While I nipped below into the fo'c's'le and started to produce mugs of hot coffee before cooking the eggs and bacon, Jack tackled the engine in the confined space between the saloon and what we had come to call the Ladies' Cabin. For some minutes he swung the handle, grunted and swore in rotation, but the Ailsa Craig was still asleep.

'My own fault,' he exclaimed. 'I ought have examined these plugs and cleaned them before turning in last night.'

Immersed in sympathy, Greg and I helped our engineer take out the plugs and heat them over one of the primus stoves. Before they were screwed back in the cylinder block I had to announce that breakfast was ready, and we decided to have it in comfort, if some haste, before getting underway: usually a good thing to do before starting on a passage.

This time the engine sprang to life at the first swing, and soon *Otter* was headed down river with the engine rumbling noisily inside its box. After washing up and stowing for sea, and making up the saloon fire until the chimney on deck began to pour a cloud of coal smoke and sparks away astern, I joined my shipmates in the cockpit. The dinghy was stowed bottom up on the starboard side deck opposite the saloon hatch which slid athwartships to port, and as we steamed slowly into the cold wind, making rather less than four knots through the water, it was something of a relief to be able to crouch together under what lee the dinghy could provide.

While the sky in the east grew steadily lighter and the giant cranes in the Dockyard passed slowly to starboard like petrified black monsters, it struck me that at this rate it was going to seem a long way down to the mouth of the river and across the widest part of the Thames mouth to the Essex shore. But as we turned into Cockham Reach the wind came a point or two free and we immediately set the mainsail and jib. *Otter* acknowledged this by bustling happily through Short Reach and past Gillingham causeway with the engine more or less freewheeling. Then sheets had to be hauled taut in again to weather Darnett Ness in Pinup Reach, but by degrees the saltings and low shores on both sides of the Medway, looking bleak in the extreme in this morning greyness, passed steadily astern.

Once through Kethole Reach with some more help from the engine we were able to bear away again into Saltpan, and with the staysail now set and drawing, our ship seemed to come to life as old time cutters always did when you set that fine pulling sail, and at Greg's suggestion Jack stopped the motor. It seemed peaceful once its stuttering exhaust and rumble below decks had ceased, but the little four-cylinder Ailsa Craig had made all the difference down the narrowest parts of the Medway against this persistent northerly.

With the Grain Spit martello tower to windward and the massive face of Garrison Point Fort passing to starboard we were glad to find that our ship could lay just about for the West Swin, even with this Thames ebb soaking her down to leeward all the time. Through the lee rigging two deep-laden barges were visible running towards the eastward, probably heading for the Four Fathom channel and along the Kentish coast. As we crossed their wake a mile or so astern of them their tan sails, curving against the murky sky, seemed to mark the only splash of colour above the grey sea.

'This is great,' said Jack happily as he blew into his mittened hands for warmth. 'At this rate we should fetch this tack down to Whitaker Spit and be there at least by low water, shouldn't we, Greg?'

At the tiller our skipper looked around at the sky and sniffed the breeze.

'Bit early to make any prophesies,' he said cautiously. 'This wind's veering a little all the time. I can only just lay the Mouse.'

Otter was sailing fast now, close-hauled as she was on the port tack, and it was a joy to feel the great weight and power of her under our feet as she swept her bows into the short seas, breasting them aside as though they didn't exist, and lifting and curtsying her bowsprit in unhurried rhythm. While I handed out mugs of hot cocoa to the crew a steamer, a regular old three-island tramp, slid past half a mile astern with the waves bursting in flashes of white against her bluff bows as she headed up river to pass the red hull of the Nore light-vessel. She seemed to epitomise all the trades that at that date were forever pouring in and out of London's River.

Two hours later our old cutter had worked her way by a couple of tacks into the West Swin, and the Mouse lightship was well astern. The ebb was doing its part for us and it began to look as if Jack's guess at our arriving at the tail end of Whitaker Spit around low water might be our lot. But even as I thought about our luck the wind seemed to falter, hesitate as though unable to make up its mind, and then it headed us with a savage little squall. The jib shook once before Greg at the helm could bear away, but he immediately had the ship under control, heading for the edge of the Barrow Sand. He was screwing up his eyes as he scanned the horizon to windward, and I noted how dark and threatening it looked.

'Come on, chaps,' he said quietly. 'Ready about. Will you get the stays'l down, MG, while Jack and I tuck a couple of reefs in? I think we're going to get snow out of that sky, and more wind than we want, and right in our teeth, too!'

Otter, in the manner of her type, lay as good as gold on starboard tack while Greg and Jack wrestled with luff cringle and leech tackle, dragging down the second reef, while I stifled the stiff folds of the staysail on the foredeck and secured it alongside the bitts. When together we had tied all the reef points in the loose-footed mains'l, the lee jib sheet was hauled in and *Otter,* snugly rigged now, gathered way again, we settled ourselves back in the cockpit, and in our own ways cursed this shift in the wind.

To windward, coming at us out of the black north-east, appeared to be a curtain of white reaching across the water beneath the slate-coloured sky above.

'Snow squall,' said Greg calmly. 'Take a bearing of the West Mouse, will you MG, before it gets blotted out.'

Almost before I had time to get the ancient handbearing compass out of its locker and jot down the reading, the vertical striped cage buoy had been lost in the murk astern. We were suddenly in a world of our own, a restricted, perishing cold world of driving snow and dark angry waves.

'It *would* catch us in the narrowest part of the Swin,' our skipper grumbled as we peered uselessly through the white blanket. 'We'd better not stand on too far on this tack or we'll be over the Maplins.'

Even as he spoke Jack gave a delighted shout.

'There's a buoy, under the lee bow.'

A black conical emerged from the gloom and reeled past a few yards away from our lee rigging. In the cussed manner of all buoys it slowly gyrated as we swept past so as to hide its name on its other side, but we were able to catch the letters LIN and that was enough. Ah, the Maplin, and lucky we were to have spotted it in time.

Greg put the yacht round in her usual slow sweep on to the port tack again, while the flakes of snow rustled into our ears, finding crevices up our sleeves and sending icy fingers down our necks. With nothing else in sight, the ebb well down, and the Swin channel hereabouts less than a mile wide, our skipper wisely chose to make short tacks of about ten minutes each, while as delegated navigator I tried to keep track of our estimated course on the chart. With a temporary cover to keep the chart more or less dry, and fingers too frozen to hold the pencil still, I felt my standard of reckoning would leave much to be desired in a navigation class held in a nice warm room. Still, we had no option but to continue slogging on in the teeth of this rising wind, and hope we should keep within the channel.

It really was blowing hard now, and the snow seemed thicker and more penetrating than ever. Although I had sailed in snow storms in other boats, this was the worst I had ever met when sailing: it was a true blizzard, and it made it almost impossible to peer to windward without feeling blinded. The cold, too, seemed to eat through one's clothing and freeze the hands despite our mitts, and we each took only short spells at the tiller so as to give the others a chance to sit out of the wind and get some circulation going.

'I hope,' Jack remarked lugubriously peering round, 'there're no barges or steamers bound up Swin today. We'd never see them till they were upon us!'

With slightly uneasy voices we told him not to be so pessimistic, but at the back of all our minds was the thought that there *could* be a vessel bound south through the Swin for the Thames, and she could pass within two hundred yards of us and we shouldn't see her. But we were occupied with other things, for with this short tacking it needed all three of us on deck to work the ship. There were no sheet winches aboard this old fashioned cutter; the jibsheets had merely a wire span at the clew with a pair of blocks which gave a single whip purchase to the cleat alongside the cockpit. It called for the strength of two men to haul in the sheet at each tack. There was therefore no time to allow anyone to clamber below to the galley to brew up a hot drink for all hands. We just had to stick it out.

The shortcomings of the athwartship sliding hatchway amidships became clear when our ship dived into a short sea and sent water cascading over the cabin top and the hatch. In really severe conditions offshore, I found myself imagining, with heavy water breaking aboard, it would be well nigh impossible for a man to get along the deck from the cockpit to the hatch, without letting in a lot of water, or getting his hand squeezed by the heavy hatch slide. But then, I mused, Victorian yachts with ladies' cabins were not expected to go far offshore in bad weather.

We had made eight or nine boards without sighting any other buoys, and I, for one, was beginning to wonder if I knew just whereabouts we were on the chart. It made me recall, inconsequentially a telling drawing by that great artist, Arthur Briscoe, in an early number of *Yachting Monthly* showing the cabin of a sharply heeling yacht, two anxious-looking yachting toffs of the period with their oilskinned skipper bent over a chart on the saloon table. The skipper, covering part of the North Sea with his outstretched hand, was saying: 'Well, gents, if we are where we *think* we are, we must be somewhere 'ere!'

I was only hoping that my own 'ere was somewhere in the Swin and neither too far over the Foulness side nor over the Barrow, but we were on starboard tack at the end of our ten minutes, and it was time to go about. The skipper started to put the helm down.

Then as *Otter* came up into the wind and her bows lifted over a sea we felt beneath our feet that deadly shock that we had instinctively been dreading ever since this blizzard had come down on us. It came again as our heel struck the sand a second time, bouncing us up and down on our feet, while the old cutter appeared to hang in stays with her bowsprit lifting and falling almost in the wind's eye.

All her forward way had been lost. She seemed dead in the water as though undecided what to do, and for a full minute, so it seemed, she hung in irons with the seas lifting her bow and dropping her keel on the cruel granite-hard sand.

'Back the jib!' There was insistence but no panic in Greg's voice, while he calmly reversed the tiller, holding it down against the starboard coaming as the old girl began to make a little stern way with the ebb under her transom.

Jack and I dived in one movement at the port jibsheet, and hauled in hard. The jib shook twice with a sound like pistol cracks, almost tearing the hemp rope through our frozen hands. Our ship seemed to teeter on the brink while we waited to see whether she was going to slew round to starboard and into deeper water, or pay off to port again and so drive harder onto the sands. In this weather with the steep seas running it could spell the end of this brave little ship, and we held our breaths as we hung on to the sheet with our senseless hands.

Then, praise be, the jib suddenly filled on the weather side, and while we held our grip on the bar-taut sheet like angry terriers, the yacht's head began to pay off to starboard until she was lying with the wind broad on her bow and her lee covering board awash.

'She's coming off, thank God!' It was the only time on this trip I had detected some emotion in our skipper's voice, and yet not a word did he utter about the incompetence of my navigation, which could have resulted in his losing his beloved ship. 'That was smart work with the jib sheet, fellahs. Well done.' Praise instead of recriminations.

Otter was not quite clear of the Maplins yet, for as she forged ahead in the troughs her keel struck the sand again and again, touch-and-go, touch-and-go it was, each time with less force, until at last she was free and threshing to windward once more. But we all wondered whether she had damaged herself, perhaps started a seam.

As though satisfied with its attempt to scare the pants off us, the wind began to ease, little by little, the sky overhead grew lighter by degrees, and suddenly, it seemed, the snow passed away to leeward like a drifting cloud. At the same time the faint sound of a bell came down to us on the wind.

'That'll be the Swin Middle,' said Greg, and at the same moment we caught sight of the light float a mile or so to windward of us. 'Well, now we know where we are.'

With the wind easier he and I went below, leaving Jack at the helm, and while Greg looked under the cabin floorboards to see how much water the yacht might be making, I busied myself with the galley stoves and worked up something good and hot to eat and drink, for we were all hungry by now.

'The old girl's not making anything that I can see,' said the skipper as he made up the saloon fire, 'despite the bumping she had. There's no doubt those old yards in the

West Country knew how to build to last, didn't they?'

As the afternoon wore on and the first of the flood tide started to run against us the wind had taken off sufficiently to make us shake out the reefs. Under whole mainsail and jib, therefore, we made our last board on starboard tack and stretched across the tail of the Whitaker sand in two fathoms. From there we gladly bore away up the Whitaker Channel and with the wind now dead aft ran steadily towards the low line of Shore Ends silhouetted against the evening sky.

The wind had not done with us yet. The sky in the north east was ominously black once more, and as we hustled past the Ridge the snow raced up astern, enveloping us again in its icy softness and cutting visibility down to a few yards. The wind was piping up as strongly as before, driving the flakes almost horizontally over the decks, but this time it was attacking us from astern, and with collars turned up and hands in oilskin pockets we could take this insidious envelopment with almost a smug feeling.

Otter was being pressed along with the parts of the mainsheet singing taut. It was my trick at the helm, and as I stood with an eye on the compass she was beginning to gripe so much that I was forced to fight her with a double line on the tiller.

'We're going too fast for comfort,' said Greg as he looked round at the snow astern and up at the gaff. 'Good time to scandalize the main, don't you think?'

I felt relieved when he and Jack went forward, and while Jack took up the slack in the toppinglift the skipper eased away on the peak halyards until the gaff was lying forward of the crosstrees and almost horizontal, pressed forward like a spinnaker pole. With the halyard belayed Greg then eased the tack downhaul tackle and hauled the foot of the mainsail some way up the mast.

'How's that, MG,' he called aft, 'that eased her?'

All vice had suddenly been drained out of that big mainsail, for it was spilling most of the wind now, and keeping *Otter* on her course was child's play. And with the foot of the sail hoisted the helmsman could stand and see at the same time where he was going, had the snow allowed him. This traditional method of reducing sail temporarily was one of the

137

gains to be had from the old-fashioned gaff mainsail not laced along the boom — the old loose-footed sail, in fact.

Thus on the young flood tide and with the snow in our ears we ran our distance to Shore Ends, and when suddenly the squall had passed away ahead and the sedge covered banks of the river could be made out on each side, we felt we were almost home. The wind, too, began to ease off so much that Greg soon had the gaff peaked up again; but he left the tack hoisted so that we could see the more clearly where we were going.

The deserted anchorage off Burnham waterfront lay before us, with a black mooring buoy dotted here and there like currants in a bun, and soon Greg pointed out his own mooring. He took over the helm, and while I went forward and lowered the jib — leaving the traveller at the end of the bowsprit in case, as he advised, we might need to hoist it again in a hurry — he took his ship round in a long sweep and brought her in a masterly piece of judgement to within a yard or so of the buoy. Jack neatly brought it aboard with the boat-hook, and between us we hauled in the heavy links of the ice-cold chain. *Otter* had arrived at her new home, and as Greg had promised, before daylight was over.

While we sat over our meal in the warmth of the saloon we talked of the passage we had made, of little ships and rigs and gadgets on board, and of cruising in general: yarning as yachtsmen the world over will do in the snuggery of a boat's cabin. When I expressed my regret at my careless navigation in the Swin which had put his ship on the sands, Greg only waved it aside with a cheerful grin.

'Forget it, MG,' he said. 'It was a bit dicey for a minute, I admit, but it can happen to anyone short tacking in a narrow channel, with visibility down to nil. Anyway, if you sail around these waters, running aground is just a risk that has to be accepted.'

It was generous of him, for he had relied on me as navigator and my poor reckoning had resulted in our hitting the Maplins with still some ebb to run, and if we hadn't managed to get off when we did the old *Otter* could have gone to pieces on the flood. But such risks, as he so cheerfully said, must be accepted by those who elect to sail little ships around the East

Coast, or anywhere else where shoals and sandbanks abound. It is one of the aspects of cruising that holds many of us with its fascination, for I think it can truly be said that to most cruising men any pastime or sport that has no element of risk whatever in it seems pointless, and just not worth taking up.

But, secretly, I did think after today's episode in the Swin I ought to get hold of Briscoe's drawing and hang it up on my study wall at home, if only as a reminder of life in general. 'If we are where we *think* we are . . . !'

Up Whitaker with mains'l scandalized

12

Cruising is what you make it

What is it about the East Coast, the question is so often asked, that can cast such a spell over boating men who sail in its waters. It would be difficult to find any single explanation for those who spend most of their sailing days between the North Foreland and say, Lowestoft, and speak of these waters as one of the best cruising grounds for the small boat sailor.

Yet some yachtsmen do fall under the spell of the Thames Estuary and all its adjacent coastline, and it has even been implied — in print, too — that these sandbanks and channels and creeks and swatchways share a certain *magic*. How can one explain that? Other yachtsmen who have migrated to the Thames Estuary from say, the Solent, the West Country, or the West Coast of Scotland, can be fully excused if they say they find much of these waters off the East Coast unexciting, drab and dreary with their low, featureless coastline, the expanse of sands that dry out at low water — many of them out of sight of land, even — the puzzling channels that meander between them, and the rivers with their extensive foreshores of soft glutinous mud. Why, they'll exclaim, recalling the crystal clear water off Cornwall or the landlocked anchorages amongst the Western Isles, the sea off the East Coast is so full of sand in suspension that you can't even see three feet below the surface. You can't tell how deep or shallow it is until you're already aground, while in breezy weather the whole sea takes on that muddy yellow-greenish tinge that the Van de Veldes, father and son, knew how to paint with such exquisite realism.

A newcomer to the Estuary in command of a deep draught

vessel might well regard the whole of the East Coast as a plague of a place for sailing, and if he feels apprehensive and unhappy, as so many deep water skippers have felt when navigating its waters, and he longs to sail his ship back to the deeper waters of the Channel or the West Coast, who can really blame him? Given the opportunity, most yachtsmen would choose almost anywhere else for their regular cruising ground.

That my own version of small boat cruising has had to be limited to weekends and to summer leave taken in two ten-day spells within easy reach of London, was the result of my editorial job with the *Yachting Monthly* for forty years, added to work on the drawing board in producing designs for suitable cruising yachts, and to the writing of a number of books. For all those who thus work seriously at their chosen career there is accordingly little time to spare for just barging about in boats. Long periods spent cruising (which have since become such an agreeable feature of the life pattern of successful self-employed businessmen, school teachers, university students, married couples between jobs, and State-assisted layabouts) were out of the question. Any dreams of a long voyage in one's own little ship round Britain, or to the Mediterranean, the West Indies or perhaps to the Pacific islands, had to remain dreams.

But this time-limited cruising was indeed no hardship, for I have always thoroughly enjoyed the narrow-water pilotage and boatmanship involved in exploring all the inlets and nooks and crannies of the Essex and Suffolk coasts. And I think I have already mentioned the late Francis B Cooke, who was happy to spend all his sailing life — something in the region of seventy-five years — in short cruises between Lowestoft and the Kentish coast.

It is not that other forms of cruising have never come my way, for kind friends have allowed me to crew them in other waters, and I have both enjoyed the experiences and learnt much from them. For instance, asked to try out yachts which I had designed for their owners, I sailed down Channel and around the coast of Devon and Cornwall, learning to love the anchorages and the superb scenery of the West Country. On another occasion I joined a tough traditional 35ft (10.7m) ketch of my design whose owner based her on the Clyde, and spent a fortnight in the summer of 1935, I think it was, exploring the Western Isles from Dumbarton through Crinan to Skye and the Outer Hebrides and back to Oban. As I have never sailed in Irish waters I cannot make invidious comparisons, but of the cruising areas I have sampled I consider without hesitation the West Coast of Scotland to be the most beautiful and satisfying for the soul.

Scottish yachtsmen are fortunate in having such an extensive and lovely area for cruising within easy reach of their industrial cities. The real extent of this varied cruising ground was brought home to me one evening during this cruise when we took our little ketch into yet another charming landlocked anchorage where there was one other yacht lying at anchor. She was a beautiful white 48ft (14.6m) gaff ketch from the board of that master designer Alfred Mylne, named *Ron.* She was owned by Colonel Charles Spencer, then Commodore of the Clyde Cruising Club, and author of that excellent book on ropework, *Knots, Splices and Fancy Work,* who normally spent a month or two each summer cruising around the Western Isles. Colonel Spencer was largely responsible for the Clyde C C's *Sailing Directions* which lists some hundreds of anchorages, the only known complete guide for this area. We were invited aboard that evening 'for a wee dram, maybe' and, while we sat in the mahogany panelled saloon (and what a cosy place it was for a raw Scottish evening!) Colonel Spencer told us that this season, after more than thirty years of cruising off the West Coast, he had found two more anchorages that he had never visited before.

With so much to choose from, and with superb scenery thrown in, the sailing man seeking peace and solitude can find all he needs amongst the Isles. The only fly in the ointment is the weather. For, let us face it, in between days of sunshine and light breezes there are more likely to be weeks of bad weather as one depression after another rides in from the Atlantic. Scotch mists — by which the hardy Scots mean a cold driving rain — are notorious on this coast, and those yachtsmen who would explore the Western Isles in their little ships must expect to find this kind of weather, with its depressing lack of visibility, for much of the time. One can be (in fact we were, when anchored in the Outer Hebrides) weatherbound and unable to escape for two or three days on end, while the perishing blasts from the Atlantic drive across the rainwashed rocks and cause even the heather to cringe. Those whose claim is for a place in Paradise must surely pay a price, and the price to be paid for all the glories of Western Isles cruising must often be the Scottish weather.

As a complete contrast, a few years before the War I took my summer holiday at Christmas and spent ten days with an old sailing friend who represented an English firm in Lisbon and kept his boat on the Tagus. She was a pretty little 29ft (8.8m) varnished teak gaff cutter named *Cherub*, which had been built by Summers and Payne at Southampton in 1898 — and I believe is still afloat, back in England. The weather with its blue skies and light breezes was like spring in England, and we planned to explore the upper reaches of the river, sailing in company with another friend who owned a true American catboat.* This was a distinctive broad, flat lapstrake-built centreboarder, 25ft (7.6m) long with 12ft (3.7) beam, with its mast, as in all the Cape Cod cats, stepped just abaft the straight stem. There was a big gaff mainsail with its boom end a few feet beyond the broad transom stern, no headsail of any kind, a barn door of a rudder, and a big wooden centreboard whose case divided the cabin down the middle. She had no motive power beyond her one sail and a springy sweep.

Above Lisbon the Tagus opens out to such width that no land appears above the horizon on the other side of the river: it looks as if you are putting out to sea instead of heading up river. There were creeks with treacherous mussel banks which had to be watched, and great stretches of sand with winding creeks and shallow swatchways between them, and we found that navigating hereabouts called for the same shoal water technique as we were used to in our own Estuary.

After one or two groundings in my friend's cutter, and one spell of seven hours lying over at an uncomfortable angle waiting for the next tide while the catboat sailed around, we had to admit how well adapted the latter boat was to this kind of ditchcrawling. While we with our five foot of draught had to work our way wisely around sand spits, he with his board up could slither over the top of them and sail way out ahead of

*For reference: Plans and account of Cape Cod catboats in *American Sailing Craft* by Howard I Chapelle (Kennedy Brothers Inc, New York, 1936).

us. And on occasion when tacking slowly in a light evening breeze, feeling our way into one of the creeks, the catboat's centreboard became a most sensitive sounding device. The board was only lightly weighted and needed neither winch nor tackle to haul it up: approaching shallow water the technique was for the helmsman to hold the tiller in one hand and the centreboard lanyard in the other. Immediately the line went slack he knew the board was skating over the bottom, and with helm down the cat spun round on to the other tack while the 'reins' became taut again until the other side of the creek was felt. It was almost automatic, more definite than the ubiquitous echo-sounder of today's yachts, and in the dark far less trying on the eyes.

In this life there are always penalties to pay for any great gains, and perfect though a Cape Cod cat might be for its original purpose as an inshore fisherman off the coast (much as the Yorkshire coble has developed for its own shore), it had its limitations. With the mast in the eyes of her and a big old-fashioned gaff mainsail, running before a fresh breeze showed what a hard-mouthed bitch she could be. The pressure on the mainsail so far forward, even if it was double reefed, pushed her bow right down, while her broad stern rose, lifting the great rudder half out of the water, so that the helmsman had to struggle and sweat to hold her from broaching-to. Hauling the board right up helped a little, but she could still play tricks before a strong following wind, and *could* get completely out of control.

Under the same conditions the old *Cherub* with her thoroughbred lines and well-balanced hull ran straight and true, rolling her boom end into the water now and again, perhaps more than somewhat, but keeping to her course down wind with but one hand on her tiller. An American catboat is no sort of vessel to make long offshore voyages with her exhausting antics in any sort of sea and an inability to lie hove-to. But for dodging about sandbanks in shallow estuaries a catboat can be great fun and very safe.

During our cruise in company we were able to watch a constant stream of local craft under sail, for Portugal was still a poor country for most of its people, and the fishermen and local trading shipowners had not run to motors for their craft as yet. The most common type seen was the sailing *fregatta*, flat bottomed with chines, about 50ft to 60ft (15m to 18m) in length, with a high curved stem which was attributed to the influence of those wonderful seafarers of the ancient world from the Levant, the Phoenicians, who had settled in the Tagus before Julius Caesar invaded Britain. The hulls of these shapely barges were decorated with colourful and elaborate designs, while their most noticeable feature was the mast which raked aft about twenty degrees. This enabled it to act as a derrick when the main halyard block was used for hoisting cargo. With their short gaff mainsails and large foresail set at the stemhead they had some resemblance to the Dutch botter as they sailed up and down the Tagus laden with fish or wine casks, cork or bricks, ox hides or timber or a variety of other cargoes. Distinctive as the wine boats of the Douro farther north, the Tagus *fregattas* were an animated and colourful reminder of the days of commercial sail.

What, then, it has so often been asked, *is* the best kind of boat to buy for cruising on the East Coast? There is, needless to say, no simple answer to this one, for selecting the most suitable boat for someone else is no easier than choosing him the best car, the best house, or the best job. It is so very much a matter of opinion and of personal preferences. One can only review what the new owner intends to do with his boat, make one or two suggestions, and leave him to make the final decision.

Assuming that your way of boating will be to cruise in an unhurried manner, even just to potter about the coast, and that you have no urge whatever to compete in either class or handicap racing, then those contemporary racing sloops you will have admired, glistening in all their glory at successive Boat Shows, are not to be even considered. With their hulls strangely moulded by the handicapping rules into the shape of giant orange pips, with a narrow and deep fin keel and a separate rudder, these yachts are designed solely for racing and are high performance sailers excellent for the racing owner — but not quite suitable for the modest cruising man.

Amid the dazzle and excitement of a Boat Show, slick salesmen might try to get you to believe that, because some of these highflyers have accommodation with berths for six or seven they will make excellent cruising yachts for the family, but you need not believe this. Not many of these gimlet-eyed gentlemen ever sail in a yacht at sea, and they might not even know how difficult it can be to steer some of these fin and dagger rudder yachts in breezy conditions on a coastal passage. Neither are they likely to mention to you that in cruising any estuary waters in the world it is inevitable that, sooner or later, a yacht will go aground. If this, as so often happens, occurs on a falling tide on a rock-hard sand bank, the mind boggles at what may happen to such a boat.

A fin keel racing yacht with deep draught is, therefore, not intended for sand navigation and cruising adventures. The first essential, then, for our type of boat is that she must be able to take the ground, whether hard or soft, without damaging herself, and also without lying so far over as to risk filling on the next tide before she picks up and floats. This implies a yacht with a beamy hull and a moderate draught. And if we have in mind taking short cuts across the sands on a rising tide (take great care if it is falling!), using shallow swatchways and channels such as the Rays'n, and working in and out over river bars like that at Woodbridge Haven or Orford Haven with perhaps only four feet at low water, a foot or so of draught one way or the other can be important.

Many artificial yacht harbours offer problems to a yacht with deep draught, for most marinas have a sill at the entrance so as to keep a desired level inside the harbour at low water, and the time before or after high water that a yacht can enter or leave will depend critically on her draught. Another problem at some excavated yacht marinas is a persistent silting-up of berths and entrance channels, and sometimes a yacht of deep draught — two metres or so — can have difficulty in getting to a berth, or finding one at which she will be afloat at all states of tide.

It is for reasons such as these that firms manufacturing cruising production yachts are increasingly concentrating on boats of quite moderate draught, and in many cases boats with twin bilge keels which can be relied upon to take level ground upright, as when cruising to harbours that dry out. The long legged craft is here at a disadvantage leaning against the quayside with safety lines rigged aloft (which require to be tended as she settles or lifts on the tide), and a boat that comfortably squats on the ground can be a great solace to her skipper and crew.

As in all things there are both good and bad examples of twin bilge keel yachts. A well-proportioned and soundly constructed bilge keeler can be very good indeed, with a sailing performance as good as many a centreboarder or keel boat of her type; but alas, the explosion in boating recreation tempted many small firms to try their hand at producing cheap boats, and with little knowledge of the sea and hardly any of boatbuilding techniques some of these firms created some bad examples of the blown-up soap dish variety, and helped to give twin keelers in general a tarnished reputation. Happily few of these firms stayed the course, and in due time good design and quality prevailed; but in selecting a twin bilge keel boat, therefore, it pays the newcomer to study the yachting magazine sailing reports and to heed advice to shop around.

If your boat is to be kept on a mooring which dries out at low water, or may take the ground for the night when you are cruising and exploring the upper reaches of some creek, thought should be given to the toilet facilities. Once the water has left her your little ship's traditional sea toilet with its pump-through arrangement cannot be used. Here the chemical toilet comes into its own, and as harbours and whole rivers in various parts of the world are increasingly affected by local anti-pollution laws, it seems likely that the sea-flushing toilet will soon be a luxury of the past and self-contained toilet arrangements obligatory in all yachts.

How big should be the boat depends on the wealth of the owner, how many in the crew to help him sail her, where he intends to keep her, and how much comfort on board is considered essential for tranquillity and not too much sulking amongst the family. Remember, the bigger the boat the deeper will be the draught, and accordingly the fewer the places available to her. For years I found my little bawley-type cutter *Storm* quite adequate for my modest cruising needs. She measured 26ft (7.93m) on deck with 9ft (2.74m) beam and a draught aft of 3.25ft (1.0m). Because of her smack-type features and inside ballast her headroom was low, and I should find it very trying today. On the other hand, *Nightfall*, which followed on later, was 31ft (9.45m) on deck with the same beam and draught as *Storm*'s. But with an outside iron ballast keel of two tonnes, higher topsides, and a well-arched coach-roof she had 5ft 9in (1.75m) headroom under the beams (more under the central skylight) and a great deal of comfort for a yacht of her size. For sailing about the East Coast I found her on the whole an excellent type of boat.

Whatever size or style of boat is chosen for cruising of this kind I consider high on the list of priorities the boat's ability to look after herself in a hard blow when her crew might be incapacitated by seasickness, exhaustion or sheer fright — as has happened to most of us in our time. For me a good cruising boat is one that will stay on course with no one at the helm when sailing in reasonable weather; and in really hard conditions will lie quietly hove-to with jib or stays'l a-weather, mainsheet eased a little, and the tiller held by its line to lee-ward: or if wheel steered, then with the wheel becketted in the same position to suit the individual boat.

This implies a yacht with a traditional underwater profile, having a rounded forefoot which is not too much cut away, and a long keel reaching aft to the heel of the rudder, which it should protect on grounding. Yachts of this so-called old-fashioned type give one a feeling of great confidence and power when you leave them to look after you, a feeling that the old boat knows what she is doing, even if the weather doesn't. The crew are far less likely to become exhausted than if they have been taking it in turns to sail a fin keeler which sheers about all over the place like an excited puppy on a lead.

If the boat you buy, however, happens to be of the contemporary kind with a short keel and proves, as expected, a lively creature to keep on course in a breeze of wind and a following sea, then for passage-making and for the comfort of the crew, the adjustable tiller line will not be enough. Some form of self-steering device will obviously be advisable.

There are numerous mechanical wind-vane operated steering gears on the market; some are more ingenious and complicated than others, but all offer a degree of automatic control over the average sailing yacht which can relieve the crew of much helmsman fatigue during a cruise. Some owners, having more money than even they know what to do with, are never content until their boats are fitted with all the fascinating electronic devices available to the modern 'with-it' yachtsman. On board some modern fully equipped yachts you may expect to find wind speed and direction indicators, course simulators and correctors, automatic speed and distance run electric logs, rigging tension recorders, fail-safe navigation lights, gas detectors and automatic extractors, self-operating fire extinguishers, radio telephone ('must tell the wife we've arrived'), echo sounders with depth recorder warning lights or horn in shoaling water, radio direction finders (RDF) and, of course, automatic steering. Let's face it, all this is very good for trade.

This last electronic gadget is possibly the most valuable of all the foregoing marvels of science, for it enables the skipper/navigator to set the course by the compass and to leave the yacht to go merrily on her way, while the crew get some sleep or go about their daily chores. It was the auto-steerer that made possible such events as the Single-handed Transatlantic and the Round the World yacht races, while with it single-handers and yachts with minimal crews are able to make long ocean voyages with little steering fatigue. On the reverse side of the coin, however, the autopilot has also enabled big ships to stay exactly on course with no one at the wheel and — let it be admitted — often with nobody even looking out. That is an aspect of the highly sophisticated electronic age in which we live which can on occasion cause great anxiety to the yachtsman in his little boat when slowly crossing a busy shipping lane.

Another question which occasionally crops up when cruising on the East Coast is being discussed is: what is the best rig for this kind of coastal pottering and creek crawling? Once again there is no easy and quick answer, for much will depend on the kind of boat in mind. The contemporary racer with a strip of mainsail and a variety of masthead jibs of different sizes is highly efficient and fast, provided you have a crew who can be relied upon to hand and change jibs smartly when wind conditions dictate. On the other hand, for the man sailing alone, or with a wife and young family who are as yet unable to help him with deck work and sail changing, this racing type sloop rig is anything but handy in changeable conditions. If however the headsails are divided into a masthead jib and a staysail set on an inner forestay — turning the yacht into a stemhead cutter — then sail can be reduced easily, when a squall sweeps over the ship, by dropping either the jib or the staysail. If in addition the jib, instead of running on hanks on the masthead stay, has a roller furling gear (either the old Wykeham Martin or one of the much more expensive modern gears) it can be furled from the cockpit, and this can be a great blessing for the single-hander in blustery weather or the approach to an anchorage.

Some yachtsmen ask whether gaff rig wouldn't be handier than contemporary sail plans. There are good arguments for a well-proportioned gaff rig aboard a suitable hull. And in boats of the smack type with a long straight keel the gaff mainsail set loose-footed (with a boom, but not laced along it) has many points of convenience for the single-hander, as I think I have mentioned in this book. The sail can be set without difficulty when, for instance, running out of a narrow creek against the first of the tide with the wind right aft; in a sudden squall sail can also be temporarily shortened by setting up the toppinglift and tricing the tack up the mast; in reducing speed, say, on the approach to an anchorage, the gaff can also be settled with the peak halyards eased, so as to scandalise the mainsail and spill most of the wind from it.

In short, the old-fashioned gaff mainsail can be more versatile than the Bermudian, even though it loses when hard on the wind. With its blocks and tackles, its miles of rope, and the hounds and crosstrees and ironwork on the mast, it is without doubt far more picturesque than the jib headed sail. Photographs of the start of any yacht race today, showing the competitors as almost identical triangles of white, appear insipid against those splended pictures of Kirk and Beken and Douglas Went of old time yachts racing with their individual rigs and great jackyard topsails. Thanks to author and yacht designer John Leather and his two charming books of photographs, *Gaff Rig* (Adlard Coles, 1970) and *A Panorama of Gaff Rig* (Barrie and Jenkins, 1977), today's gaff enthusiasts can enjoy studying rigging details of the past in all their complexity.

In my own limited experience I have enjoyed handling

boats under a variety of rigs, and have found many points both for and against all rigs under different conditions. The last gaff rigged yacht I owned, *Nightfall*, had a simple mainsail with a roller reefing boom, a short light gaff, and lightweight cotton sails, and her mainsail was never any problem to whip up or down. It is over forty years since I sold her, and I have never *owned* a gaff rigged boat since, but I have sailed with many friends with gaff sloop, cutter, yawl, and ketch rigs. From what I have been able to discover there seems little to choose between them for the lone sailing man who wants to explore the creeks and rivers of the East Coast, or anywhere else where seas and tidal conditions are similiar. Much will depend on the type of boat and the skipper's own ability, for as the age old saying has it,

Ships is all right, it's the men wot's in 'em.

Perhaps I can best close this chapter with a little incident of a contemporary kind. We were creeping up on the tide, my shipmate and I, past the spherical buoy with the topmark that points the way into the Walton channel, with a light easterly breeze astern and still some more flood tide to run. I was reflecting that it must be fifty years almost to the day since another schoolfriend and I had set out from Ipswich for our first ever foray in our newly acquired, but in fact very old, 6-ton cutter. It had been during that intensely hot summer of 1921, and in our woeful ignorance of how to handle a yacht of *Undine*'s size we had soon gone aground, and had spent the next few hours lying on our side in misery, while the black ooze around us dried and steamed in the sun.

Now, half a century later, more knowledgeable perhaps, but doubtfully any wiser, I was learning the feel of my latest boat *Kylix* as we ran slowly up the broad reach of Hamford Water. *Kylix* was, heaven help me, my twenty-first boat and I had designed her after retirement from London as an old man's single-hander. Her mooring was off Kyson Point below Woodbridge, where I was then living, and drawing less than one metre with her centreplate hauled up she could lie afloat at low spring ebb. Just over 8m (27ft) in length, she was light and easy to handle, being rigged as a Bermudian cutter with

Wykeham Martin furling jib; and her 15hp diesel was powerful enough to enable her to punch her way around the coast
against a strong wind if necessary. She seemed to me to have
all the attributes of a well-behaved cruising boat at home in
estuary waters.

After watching through the glasses the colony of
screaming black-headed gulls gyrating above their nesting
sites on the Horsey Island saltings, Philip turned to me.

'Where do you intend to bring up,' he asked. 'In Kirby
Creek, if there's room?' And he nodded at the small crowd of
yachts at anchor at the head of the West Water, the local
fishermen's name for this stretch of Hamford.

Quiet evening in Kirby Creek

It certainly did look a little too crowded for another boat
to anchor, although they appeared at a glance to be only small
craft with a great similarity in their white plastic hulls, plain
sloop rig, and inflatables, like black American doughnuts,
hauled close up to the sterns. As the entrance to the creek
opened up to port between the eastern end of Horsey and
Skipper's island it, too, appeared to be filled with a packed
row of yachts and motor cruisers.

In near silence *Kylix*, as we hauled the sheets for the wind
on the beam, slid past the yachts one by one, and we were
relieved to see one space between two of the boats where we
could round up and let go our anchor for the night. But we
should have to continue on to the head of the creek where it
widened out to give us room to gybe round.

As our boat swept round with helm up we had a glimpse
of the wide expanse of Horsey Mere where, now covered by
the tide, the causeway called the Wade is the island's only link
with the mainland. These places were well known to the late
Arthur Ransome in his little ketch *Peter Duck*, for his
charming books must have introduced hundreds of young
families to these *Secret Waters*. Yet this area of meres and mud
flats, of rotting posts and withies waving in the tide, of creeks
that meandered mysteriously behind sedge covered islets, and
of the pungent smell of seaweed mingled with the cries of
waders feeding along the tideline, is not so remote from
civilisation. Less than two miles away the houses of Walton
stand in rows like monuments to a Victorian seaside town with
their windows turned seaward, while over the greensward of
the Naze the old tower overlooks a huddle of newer houses as
it guards the approach to Harwich and the busy dock complex
of Felixstowe and Parkeston Quay.

Half way down the creek *Kylix* carried her way quietly
into the only space we had noticed between the yachts and
dropped her anchor close to the weather shore. This was one
of my earliest favourite anchorages, I mused, as we stowed our
sails, and later as we sat in the cockpit watching the tide creep
up towards the banks we both felt a great contentment. There
was no other place we would rather be.

A faintly persistent murmur of an outboard engine
became louder as a bright red speedboat appeared round the
point and headed down the creek.

'Ere y'are, Bert,' shouted a rough voice. 'Good spot this.
Do a treat.'

With sinking hearts we watched the three figures in black
wet suits prepare the skis while they bawled at one another
and one of the figures emitted girlish shrieks. In a minute they
were away, roaring down towards the mouth of the creek with
the girl skier in tow.

'Thank goodness,' Philip remarked in a low voice as if they might hear him, 'they've got the whole of Hamford Water to ski in, and . . . oh no, not *another* one!'

In the roar of the red boat's outboard we had not noticed the approach of a second speedboat, a white one this time. In a few minutes these sportsmen, two men and two girls like black demons in their wet suits, had rigged up their skis and in a frenzy of shouting roared after the first lot.

For a time there was peace on the water and we sat enjoying the scent of the may blossom in a hedgerow just over the seawall, and could hear the neighing of a horse in the meadows, and I recollected that the farmer was breeding horses with an Arabic strain on the island.

'Would you believe it, Maurice,' Philip's tone was one of astonishment. 'Those so-and-so's are coming back!'

Headed by the red gang the two speedboats came roaring past a few yards away with the two skiers skilfully weaving across each other's wake as the boats headed up past the rows of moorings. In turn each yacht jigged and danced in their wash, while the skiers turned at the head of the creek and roared past again, only to come round near the mouth of the creek and go through the thrill of weaving in and out of the yachts once more. There was more than dismay on the faces of people who sat watching the display aboard some of the other yachts, but the speedboat men and their skiers appeared oblivious of the anger they were causing.

Philip is a skilled wild fowler, and the instinct to bring down a flighting duck with on barrel showed at this moment in the expression on his face as he stood up and glared at the zooming black figures.

'By gad,' he muttered, 'if I had my twelve bore with me right now I'd let 'em have both barrels up the backside!'

For the next hour and a half, until the sun set behind the trees and the tide had begun to fall, the two parties continued to enjoy their noisy sport up and down the creek, while the yachts rocked in their wash and I began to wonder if my old shipmate was going to have an apoplectic fit. Then at last, after much shouting to one another, the sportsmen roared away for home, and peace descended upon the scene once more.

Nobody, we assured ourselves, wanted to stop other people from enjoying their chosen sport, but this display of callous ignorance was too much to bear in silence. The shiny trailer-boats were clearly quite new, recently acquired toys perhaps, and as great a status symbol outside a home in a housing estate as a Jag used to be. Their owners, we felt, could not belong to any waterski club, where rules of conduct are laid down and usually faithfully kept by their members. Yet, what could anyone aboard any of the boats in the anchorage have done? Call out at the skiers, and they can't hear you; show gestures of displeasure, and they accept them as applause of their undoubted skill; write to the Press ('Disgusted, of Kirby Creek') and they might never read a newspaper, nor even look at a boating journal.

'If I'd had my gun . . .' Philip repeated under his breath, and I was forced to chuckle at the thought that his remedy would undoubtedly be noticed, if only temporarily.

But as we sat and enjoyed our sundowners, the annoyance was soon forgotten. Above the silence of the evening we became aware of many familiar little sounds: the soft gurgle of the ebb flowing past the anchor cable, the hissing of countless worm holes along the water's edge, the plop of a grey mullet breaking the surface, the hysterical 'pee-pee-pee' of an oyster catcher wheeling past, a flash of black and white, and the sudden 'craak' of an old heron standing sentinel somewhere over there on the saltings. With Philip and his cousin Tom and other old shipmates I have lain at anchor in these creeks at different times of the year and known the breeze off the land come laden with the heady scent of a field of beans, the fresh smell of rain-washed marram grass, or the childhood memory of freshly mown hay and threshing time.

In comparison with noise-making sports like motorcycle racing, football, speedboating, or even private flying, it is not necessarily a holier-than-thou attitude to think of small boat sailing and cruising as a form of pleasure that need cause no inconvenience to others. With your little home about you, and the warm lamplight in the cabin inviting you below when the evening air begins to feel chilly, you have with you everything a man or woman may need to feel at peace with a world which at such times can seem far, far away.

156

And if I tell you that, after more than fifty years of sailing, I still find this a bewitching hour as the sun goes down, and that I still experience a feeling of magic in these quiet and seemingly remote anchorages on such a night, then I can only say Go, brave sailorman, and see for yourself in your little ship, and to you,

Good Cruising!